Discipleship Books:

The Son

By

Philip Watson

Book 2

of the Trinity Series

ISBN 978-0-473-30765-3

Dedication

Dedicated to my loving wife Dianne, and my three children, Andrew, Jonathon and Ruth.

My grateful thanks for allowing me to spend so much of my spare time writing these words.

Acknowledgments

My grateful thanks to Warren Portsmouth who patiently helped me review the manuscripts of my books. Warren suggested improvements and asked questions at appropriate points.

I also want to acknowledge the help of the Holy Spirit for inspiring me to write these books and for frequently reminding me of scriptures, relevant to topics, in each book.

7.94

Discipleship Books by Philip Watson

The Jesus Series:

Jesus The Ministry

Jesus The Incarnation

Jesus Changed Our Lives

The Trinity Series

The Father

The Son

The Holy Spirit

Other Books

The Cross and The Triangle

Successful Relationships

101 Spiritual Principles

1000 Great Quotes

Great Summaries

Contents

Introduction

Most Christians desire to be like Jesus. God has that desire too, ...for us to be conformed to the image of his Son. Romans 8:29. With the idea of finding the image of Jesus, I walked into a Christian book shop to find the section about Jesus.

I was expecting to find, rows and rows of books about Jesus, because he is after all:

> The Son of God Rom 1:4
>
> The Messiah John 1:41
>
> The head of the Church Eph 1:22.
>
> The author and perfecter of our faith Heb 12:2.
>
> The way and the truth and the life.... John 14:6

And there are so many other titles given to Jesus such as Savior and Christ and collectively these titles suggest that our Christian book shops should be, 'full' of books about Jesus! However, in this bookshop, I was unable to find even one book about him.

Thinking that it was because of the 'very limited range' of books in the first Christian book shop, I went to another Christian book-shop to find the rows and rows of books about Jesus - but it was the same story!

There were no books about Jesus, the head of the Church, the Savior of the world, the Son of God and I soon began to ask myself questions like. Where are the rows of books about Jesus, the "head of the Church", the Messiah, "the author and perfecter of our faith".

There were books on personal growth, spiritual growth and church growth. There were books about most issues and situations in life. There were books about divorce, marriage, singleness, sexuality, and health. There were books about Bible characters and modern-day saints. Every subject it seemed except Jesus, the Son of God - the founder of the the Church.

But all was not lost. While still at the second

Christian bookshop and about to leave, I finally did find some books about Jesus! Of course, they were in childrens section!

Naturally, that got me thinking. Do we only write books and teach about Jesus, in Sunday School or whatever the childrens program is called in each Church?

After that I began to list some possible reasons why there are no books about Jesus, written specifically for adults?

Maybe many Christians are like me, and consider they know all there is to know – about Jesus. Many learned about Jesus in Sunday School (or whatever the childrens program was called in their Church), and consider they know all there is to know about him. It is simple.

Jesus (the Son of God) came to this earth as a baby. He was conceived in Mary's womb by the Holy Spirit. He grew up as a child in Nazareth, and became a carpenter. Then at about the age of thirty, he began a ministry of teaching, of healing, of deliverance and love.

 And then, after having trained up twelve disciples, left this earth after an unjust and cruel death, to become our Lord and Savior.

End of story. End of book! Well I hope not.

Surely there is more that can be written about Jesus than that, brief summary?

But that was one possible reason for there not being any books about Jesus. We adults consider we know, all there is to know, about him.

There is perhaps another reason why there have been so few books about Jesus, written specifically for adults. We modern-day disciples sometimes find it hard to relate Jesus' world, to our world: i.e. For most Christians, there are no lepers in their immediate vicinity and there are no Pharisees,dressed in long robes who we can accuse of being hypocrites. And there are not many people we could conclusively say – that person is, demon possessed!

So maybe that is another reason there have so few books about, the Son of God and the savior of the World? His world and our world, seem, unconnected!

There may be other reasons. The way Jesus is portrayed and the way his teachings are presented. First of all, the way he is portrayed. His manner. Jesus is portrayed in the Gospels as being a person focused exclusively on love and truth and the kingdom of God. And in that presentation, there are no images of Jesus, say smiling, or being playful,

I am saddened by that portrayal because I am sure Jesus did both, and often! It is just that the Gospel writers did not record those occasions and personal details like that.

For that reason I am glad that on the front cover of the book titled *The ministry of Jesus,* Jesus is pictured smiling. As for being playful, particularly with children, there is circumstantial evidence that he was playful with children.

After the disciples had been disputing who was the greatest, Jesus held a child close to him and said, "Whoever welcomes one of these little children in my name, welcomes me... "Mark 9:37 This took place in a house Mark calls "the house".

A house scholars believe was the house where Jesus based himself during the three years of his ministry and which some speculate was, Peter's house. Because Bible scholars have identified three ministry trips that suggests that much of the time Jesus was based at this house.

And during that time, I suggest he played with the children and talked to them. In the brief account in Mark's Gospel, our picture is that

Jesus took a child who was familiar and comfortable with Jesus, and that is why this child stood there, while Jesus made a point to the adult disciples.

Then there is the way his teachings are presented. They are presented as, as short, sharp, doses of truth. Sometimes too short and too sharp, for many!

I mean who wants to read the teachings of a prophet/teacher who asks his disciples to take up their cross and follow him when they could read passages like the following. One which emphasizes our status and our blessings.

"Praise be to the God and Father of our Lord Jesus Christ, who has blessed us in the heavenly realm with every spiritual blessing. For he chose us.. In love he predestined us to be adopted..." Eph 1:3-5

Whatever the reason or reasons for there being no books about Jesus in our Christian bookshops, written for adults (and which honor* him) – that was all the more reason to attempt writing a book about Jesus. But where to start?

*Some have written books that represent him as a renegade, zealot and revolutionary which I suggest misrepresent Jesus.

Before beginning to write this book, as far as humanly possible, I tried to put aside the conditioning of my Church past so that I could see Jesus, and hear Jesus speaking from the pages of the Gospels, for who he was - not for who I would like him to be.

I also wanted to come to the Gospels afresh, with this simple question and this simple prayer.

> *Jesus. When I look at the Gospel records what do I notice about you and the way you conducted your ministry, that speaks to us, today?*

So before I began to put any thoughts onto my computer, I sat down in front of the Gospels with this prayer, and this attitude.

'Lord hit me afresh'. I and others have consigned you to the childrens section of our minds, and to a world of 2000 years ago. Further, you live in a room of my mind, and hat room has a sign over the doorway leading into it. And on that sign, are these words.

KNOWN INFORMATION

The result of that prayer and reflection was not a deep theology. Just a picture of the Son of God who was refreshingly different in the way he began his religious movement

It was a ministry without preference for one person, over the other.

And the God of Jesus was real, and not hidden away behind, hundreds of laws.

And Jesus was real was a real person – and not hidden away in some remote religious community. People could touch him and he touched by him. They could ask questions of him and yes - dispute with him.

And children were so incredibly important.

And when he taught, the emphasis was not on, do not, but – do and the reasons for doing. The focus of his teachings were on the attitudes that precede, the actions.

And for Jesus, his spirituality was incredibly natural. He did not have to be in the Temple to pray. A house or a street or a hillside, were just as good.

And Jesus did not consider any problem so great, that his God could not solve it. Or any sickness, beyond cure. And any person, beyond redemption. Or any person, beyond loving.

And there was another surprising picture that emerged. Jesus was so astute in everything he did. He came with goals and mission statements. And his teaching were in parables (relevant stories) And he asked questions, to get people thinking about their answers. Jesus assessed the most effective means of communication, with both individuals and groups.

And when Jesus started his religious movement, he began it by asking the future disciples to, "Come. Follow me." What a way to start a religious movement. A method so simple, and yet, so, profound! Was that because Jesus valued relationships over religious laws and rituals?

Reflection 'after this book was complete
The main focus of this book is the person of Jesus. Who he was as a person (and not his teachings) however, once I began to focus on his life and ministry, I soon began to realize that this was one egg where I could not separate the yoke from the egg-white and that both his teachings and the life he lived, go hand in hand.

So while the focus of this book, is the life he lived, rather than his teachings - inevitably, some of his teachings are woven into that picture of his life for as readers will also discover in the final chapter. What he said and what he did, are one and the same - and that for me, is one more reason to, be one of his followers.

Even though his teachings form the lesser part of this book and that was intentional, there is a chapter that focuses on his teachings titled *Do you understand Jesus?* While reading that chapter readers will discover there is a key to understanding, virtually all of his teachings.

Readers also need to understand that the focus of this book is Jesus during the three years of his ministry on this Earth and is not about his existence in heaven, prior to coming to this Earth. Nor is this book about his life in heaven, after he ascended again.

But even though Jesus' prior existence in heaven is scarcely mentioned in this book, his three years of ministry and his life on Earth, can only be reviewed in awe against the background he came from. John 1:1-3 & 14.

The change in status from one to the other, was incredible! In heaven, he had legions (a legion numbered around 6000) of angels at his command.

By contrast, on earth, though he experienced the support of his disciples (most of the time), there was significant indifference and opposition. And included among those who opposed him were. Satan, his family, his town folk and most of the religious authorities.

So to go from an existence in the glorious presence of God with thousands of angels at your command to one where family, towns folk and most of the religious authorities opposed him – was a huge change in status.

And Jesus' prior existence in heaven with the glory of God all around and with angels at his command has to be contrasted with his earthly ministry.

When Jesus began his ministry, he moved to the village of Capernaum and based himself in a house, which Mark simply calls, "the house". Mark 9:33 And when Jesus began his ministry from that house, it is likely that he brought, little more than his clothes. So our picture is this.

The co-creator of the Universe, started his ministry on the dusty roads of a backwater of the Roman Empire (Judea) disowned by his family, and owning nothing more than, the clothes he stood in.

As someone wrote about that period of his life.

"He owned everything and yet owned nothing." Amazing!

It is my hope and prayer that readers will find something fresh about Jesus in the pages of this books, and that you will find reasons to (if you have not already done so), make Jesus the author and finisher of your faith. To make Jesus: your Lord, your life, your way and your end.

God bless you.

Philip Watson.

Some bald facts about Jesus ministry.

- Began his ministry approximately 27 A.D and died, 30 A.D.

- Jesus ministry occurred during the reigns of Caiaphas the High Priest, Herod the Tetrach and Pontius Pilate (the Roman Governor)

- He called twelve men to be his closest disciples at the beginning of his ministry but the number of disciples, both female and male, grew rapidly, from there on.

- He is recorded as doing 34 miracles but in fact did many more miracles than that. The details of the other miracles, were not recorded in the Gospels - see John 20:30

- He taught 24 parables and one scholar who analyzed everything Jesus said and concluded that Jesus spoke about, 300 different subjects.

Chapter 1

Three Images of Jesus

To kick-start this book about Jesus, three images emerged, as I looked at him afresh - in the pages of the Gospels.

Image one

Jesus was 'naturally spiritual' or, 'spiritual naturally'. He knew we humans are made up of four component parts. Our heart or soul, our body, our mind and our spirit. His last words were. "Father! In your hands I place my spirit."* Luke 23:46 (G.N) When his physical body had died, his spirit lived on. But during his time on Earth his spirit was in touch with God his Father and the Holy Spirit – and his mind/heart and strength were dedicated to doing the will of God.

*The spiritual part of his life, was so much a part of who he was. That is why he told Nicodemus

> "no one can enter the kingdom of God unless he is born of water and the Spirit." John 3:5

Being naturally spiritual or spiritual naturally was evident in Jesus' prayer-life. A good example of this, is an occasion recorded in Luke's Gospel. Jesus was talking to his disciples when all of a sudden, he switched from a conversation with the disciples, to a conversation with God. Part way through a face-to-face conversation with the disciples, he started praying.

> "I praise you, Father, the Lord of heaven and earth.........Luke 10:21

It did not matter to Jesus that they were not in a synagogue or in the Temple. He knew he could pray to God about anything, anywhere. The Apostle Paul would later write. "Pray about everything" and at "all times." Jesus did not feel any need to go to the Synagogue or Temple to pray. He knew his Father was everywhere and knew everything so it was quite natural to start praying anywhere.

We are not told how regularly Jesus prayed but we can see from various Scriptures, that Jesus prayed regularly.

- Very early in the morning, while it was still dark, Jesus got up, left the house and went off to a solitary place, where he prayed. Mark 1:35

- One day, Jesus was praying in a certain place. Luke 11:1

- 'After he had dismissed them, he went up on a mountainside by himself to pray'. Matt 14:23

Jesus prayed before all of the significant phases of his ministry. Before the start of his ministry. Luke 4:2. Before the selection of his disciples. Luke 6:12 and before his trial and crucifixion. Luke 11:41

The importance of prayer to Jesus is also indicated by his teaching on the subject. The most significant words of Jesus on the subject of prayer are, " When you pray"..... Matt 6:7. He encouraged his disciples to 'ask' God for their needs, even though God already knew about them, Matt 7.7, and to use plain language, Matt 6:7-9.

Jesus taught them:

1. that God has the highest good of each person on his heart. Matt 7:9-11,

2. what to pray for, Matt 6:9-13,

3. to agree with others in prayer, Matt 18:19,

4. to be reconciled with others before praying, Matt 5:24,

5. to exercise faith, when they are praying Matt 21:22, and

6. to be persistent in prayer, Luke 11: 5-10

To summarize this snapshot on prayer, it appears that prayer to Jesus was 'natural', 'normal', 'necessary' - and sometimes 'nocturnal'.

- **Natural**: He was talking with the disciples, possibly beside the road, when he switched to a prayer to his heavenly Father.

- **Normal**: He is recorded praying in the morning and evening and at night.

- Necessary: By his life he conveyed that prayer was necessary. When he had major decisions to make, Jesus spent time in prayer - and it is implied that prayer to his Father, was the way he maintained the oneness he had with him.

- **Nocturnal**: At least once he prayed, all night.

Image two

Jesus loved and valued, children! Most readers will know of the occasion the disciples tried to prevent mothers bringing children to him, and that Jesus reprimanded the disciples, saying

> "Let the children come to me. Don't stop them! …….Then he took the children in his arms and placed his hands on their heads and blessed them." Mark 10:14-16 NLT

This is one of at least two occasions that Jesus lifted up little children. At least, one of two occasions that we read about. I'm sure there were many more. The other occasion that is recorded, was after the disciples had been discussing who was going to be the greatest. Then Jesus picked up a child and put the child on his knee, and told the disciples that the greatest in the kingdom had to become like this child.

Many Christians may not have considered what this example implies. It implies that the child, was totally familiar with Jesus and was so comfortable with being on his knee, that he or she did not mind Jesus lifting him or her onto his knee - despite the fact that twelve men were standing around, looking at both of them. That scene implies this had occurred regularly.

That picture of a child being totally comfortable sitting on Jesus' knee, is something that stood out to me because at one time, my wife and I lived some 700 miles/1200km away from our grandchild. We would go to see our grandchild about twice a year but when we did, though we were delighted to see him - to our grandchild, we were strangers! People to be treated warily.

When we first arrived, the expression on his little face was, 'who are you'? By the end of a week, he would gradually allow us to hold him on our knees, but if we tried to hold him on our knees before we had been there for at least five days, he would look very uncomfortable, and try to get off.

That is why the example of Jesus picking up a child and placing the child on his knee, implies that this child, was totally familiar with Jesus and was comfortable with being on his knee.

How this child came to be comfortable with

Jesus picking him or her up can be explained by putting together several other pieces of information. It appears that Jesus, after he left his home in Nazareth, went to live in a house in Capernaum. It was simply called "the house", Mark 9:33.

Some scholars speculate it was Peter's house, but who's house it was, does not really matter. It is likely that it was the house of one of the fishermen disciples, because the town was Capernaum, beside Lake Galilee.

As most of Jesus' ministry was in Galilee, it is likely that Jesus lived in that house for most of the three years of his ministry. If that is true, I can imagine Jesus playing with the children of that house and laughing with them and loving them during the many times that Jesus was not traveling on one of his mission trips. Sadly, any comments about Jesus playing with children, are not recorded in the Gospels.

We can see from his teachings, the value Jesus placed on children. He told adults not to look down on children because God has appointed angels for them in heaven. Matt 18:10 He also sternly warned adults not to lead them astray. The abuse of children is not mentioned specifically by Jesus, but I think we can assume from Jesus warning that he was very aware of it.

He also saw in these children, an innocent trust and it was that child-like trust that he wanted his disciples to recapture. A trust he had seen in the eyes of his nephews and nieces, and the children of the house he stayed in.

Those who have read the book *Heaven is for Real,* may remember that Colton, the not quite four year old whose spirit went to heaven, was emphatic that, Jesus loved children. See p 105

Image three

I have included this third snapshot because some readers at least find it hard to relate their image of Jesus, two thousand years ago, to our modern world of machines and technology. A world in which we have cars and jets and cell-phones and computers – and so pictures of Jesus holding lambs (like the pictures on the walls of various Sunday Schools I attended) seem to have, so little in common with our world today, but perhaps that is putting Jesus in a box?

First of all, Jesus did not need to use cell phones and texts to find out what people thought. He already knew what people were thinking because the Spirit of God had told him. It is only we, poor souls, who are not as sensitive to the Spirit of God as he was - who need to find out via Facebook/Twitter or texting what others are thinking, or have done.

Jesus was very focused! Now that is not a term, normally associated with Jesus in Christian books or sermons. Lover of people – yes! Teller of the truth – yes, but very focused? If that is what you are thinking, maybe we have locked Jesus into a particular mold The mold of an itinerant preacher.

The words "very focused", are usually used by graduates of business schools, about their plans. Graduates usually produce a computer generated business plan with their goals, and include mission statements and marker pegs along the way to measure progress.

Jesus was like a top graduate from a business school, nearly two thousand years before they created, business Schools!

At the beginning of his ministry, he told the disciples, His mission statement.

> The Spirit of the Lord is on me,
>
> because he has anointed me

to preach good news to the poor.

He has sent me to proclaim

freedom for the prisoners

and recovery of sight for the blind,

to release the oppressed,

to proclaim the year of the Lord's favor.

Luke 4:18-19

At other times, Jesus spoke simply about the purposes for which he had come to earth.

- For even the Son of Man did not come to be served he came to serve and to give his life to redeem many people. Mark 10.45 (G.N)

- For the Son of Man came to seek and to save what was lost. Luke 19.10

- For I have not come to call the righteous, but sinners. Matt 9.13

- The thief comes to steal and kill and destroy I have come that they might have life and have it to the full. John 10.10

Jesus knew exactly why he had come, and he was very focused on achieving those goals. Best of all, those goals characterized his ministry. Take the first goal. Jesus said he "came to serve". Servant leadership, was evident throughout his ministry. At the very end of his ministry he demonstrated servant leadership by washing the feet of the disciples.

He also said, I came "to seek and save the lost" and came to call "sinners". Because these two goals were part of his purpose, is why we read about him dining at the home of Zacchaeus (the cheating tax collector) and with immoral women.

It is one thing to have goals, it is another to see them through to the end. Early in his ministry Jesus said it was his goal was to 'finish his work' (the work that God had given him). At the end of his earthly life, Jesus was able to cry in both anguish and satisfaction. "It is finished" John 19.30

Goals for the twelve
Jesus not only had goals for himself, he also had goals for the twelve. From the start, he told the first disciples they were to become fishers of men. And among his final instructions were, they were to make disciples of all nations. Along the way he sent the twelve out on a 'trial missionary journey', so they could learn the trade so to speak.

Matthew 10. He took them aside for special staff-training sessions, like that found in John 14-16. And other times he took key leaders aside for special training. Matt 17:1

He had vision.

> "The harvest is plentiful but the workers are few," said Jesus. Matt 9:37

He also had a vision of how that harvest would be gathered in. By challenging his disciples to make the kingdom of God their first priority in life, and also by fully using what talents they had to gather in the harvest of new disciples. Jesus also had a vision of what the disciples could produce. A harvest thirty, sixty and one hundred times, what they sowed. Matt 13:9 & Matt 25:14 ff

Towards the end of his ministry, Jesus began to assess whether the disciples had reached certain marker points in their understanding so he asked them. "Who do you say I am?" Jesus wanted to know whether they had grasped who he was because there was little point in him leaving this earth, until they had grasped that truth.

A number to times He told them he would be crucified but rise again. We are not sure whether they did not believe what Jesus said or did not 'want' to believe what Jesus was telling them.

Jesus was very focused on achieving both his own goals and ensuring that the twelve disciples were trained and prepared for their future role in the Church. Jesus had begun his ministry by setting the goals of his disciples and now near the end of his ministry, he was leading the way.

Mark wrote

> "They were on their way up to Jerusalem, with Jesus leading the way." Mark 10:32

Jesus' final instructions to the disciples included a command that they take the Gospel to the whole world. Matt 28:19 To amplify this, Jesus gave his disciples a world wide vision of their tasks.

What is there in this image for modern day Christians? Firstly, Jesus understands our world. Don't leave him in Palestine two thousand years ago. He understands people then, and now.

He understood effective business principles and effective methods of communication such as story telling, which we call parables. When speaking to a large crowd he got in a boat and asked that it be moored not too far from the shore so that his voice would bounce off the water and amplify what he said.

He employed good management models, two thousand years management schools began to teach such principles. Jesus had a mission statement, defined purposes, a clear plan, and a vision for his disciples. He provided training, counseling, support and discipline as needed.

In summary, it has been said by none other than Napoleon that "... if Jesus had not existed, we would never be able to create him ..."

Jesus was naturally spiritual. Jesus loved children and he employed effective communication and business models, nearly 2,000 years before their significance was recognized.

Chapter 2

Jesus' Personal Qualities

This chapter focuses on some of Jesus', personal qualities. Other qualities of Jesus, like his love, his compassion and grace are the subject of chapter three.

Printed in a local business newspaper was an article written by a leadership training consultant about the qualities needed for a successful leader in business. He wrote

> Leadership is about vision, creativity, intuition and it's about people and relationships..... There's a perception that managers should be in ivory towers, not accessible, not warm. Look at Nelson Mandela. He is willing to be

vulnerable. If he wants to dance, he dances, he laughs. He is not concerned about image. If he's deeply moved he sheds a tear.

Like Nelson Mandela, Jesus was not concerned about image. He picked up children to bless them and talked with an immoral Samaritan woman, at a well. There were three reasons the Pharisees would never have stopped to talk with her. She was a woman. She was a Samaritan and she was immoral.

Bible scholars speculate that she had come out in the mid-day sun to avoid meeting other people because most people stayed indoors during the hottest part of the day. The Gospel writers tell us that when Jesus' disciples came back to him (after buying food) at the well and found him talking with this Samaritan woman, they were surprised!

That probably was an understatement. They were surprised that Jesus was talking to this person. A Samaritan woman and one who was possibly, immoral. None of these criteria concerned Jesus. Jesus was not concerned about his image in the eyes of his disciples, or religious teachers, or anyone else.

Like Nelson Mandela, Jesus wept and had

joy. John 11:25 & Luke 10:21 Jesus was the embodiment of what Paul would later write

> "Be happy with those who are happy and weep with those who weep." Rom 12:15 NLT

Even his enemies noticed that Jesus did not care about his image. One of them said, possibly as a form of flattery,

> "You are impartial and don't play favorites." Matt 22:16 NLT

An impartial person is not influenced by the differences between genders, races, health, and beliefs. Jesus conducted his ministry, without a concern for image.

Author Rick Joiner wrote a book and from memory it was called "The Vision". In that book he related how he went to heaven (presumably his spiritual body) and while there had a number of conversations with Jesus.

One of the insightful comments Jesus made to Rick at that time was. "The humble cannot be embarrassed."

Because Jesus was humble, he was not embarrassed that the only person able to offer him water at mid-day, was an immoral

Samaritan woman. Nor was he embarrassed that a blind man by the roadside in Jericho, would call out to him. Or mothers wanted to bring their children to him. Or that a Roman Centurion would want him to pray for his servant.

One action in particular, reminds us that Jesus was not concerned about his image. This action tells us how Jesus saw himself. During the last supper, Jesus washed the disciples feet. John 13:4-15

That Jesus, their leader washed their feet, indicates Jesus was not concerned about his image but also indicates that Jesus was sure he was the Son of God. If Jesus felt such an act was beneath his dignity as the Son of God, he never would have done it. Instead, I believe he washed the disciples feet with this attitude.

I am no more the Son of God because I am washing their feet and no less the Son of God, because I am washing their feet.

At that time, Jesus' action is likely to have left an indelible impression on his disciples for his actions tied in with his teachings about leadership. He told them that anyone who wanted to become a leader of all had to become, the servant of all.

Further, when he washed the disciples feet, he was not seeking credits from the disciples or anyone else - for he would be 'long-gone' before the wider church heard of this act.

This was not a stage-managed stunt to gain publicity like some political leaders tend to enjoy doing. There were no cameras or reporters at the last supper. The first written reports about Jesus washing the disciples feet, would only begin to circulate about 30 years after Jesus had left this Earth, when the gospels were written. Jesus actions suggest that he lived, as if,

he had, nothing to lose, hide or gain.

That is freedom! Jesus talked about freedom. Freedom is to live by whatever values a person has, without worrying about what others think, do or say. Freedom is to be the person we are.

If we live like Jesus and are not concerned about our image, we will be free to express our concerns, to show our sorrow or happiness. We will be free to associate with anyone we wish to, knowing God loves everyone.

Two other noticeable qualities
The old Apostle John wrote his Gospel some

40 to 50 years after Jesus' death and resurrection. Because John wrote his Gospel so long after Jesus' resurrection, by then he would have been familiar with what Mathew, Mark and Luke had written and it appears that in his Gospel, John made a point of including and emphasizing aspects of Jesus life and teachings, that the other three had missed out.

So when John sat down and wrote his gospel, what did he think the others had omitted, and required emphasizing?

In the first chapter of his Gospel, John wrote,

> "The law came through Moses. Grace and truth came through Jesus Christ." 1:17

John made a contrast between Moses and Jesus. The law of Moses was primarily a set of "do nots", while Jesus teaching was primarily a set of "do's."

His set of "do's" were preceded by the words "Happy" or "Blessed." "Blessed are those who hunger and thirst for righteousness". Other translations use the word "happy are those who ....".

These two qualities, grace and truth, that John identified as being characteristic of Jesus, are strange partners because human beings tend to emphasize, one or the other. Either grace (undeserved love) or truth, but not often both.

An example of how Jesus managed to incorporate 'both' of these qualities into his ministry to people, is illustrated by the way he handled this situation.

'The teachers of the law and the Pharisees brought to Jesus a woman caught in adultery. The Pharisees said to Jesus, "Teacher, this woman was caught in the act of adultery. In the law Moses commanded us to stone such women. Now what do you say?"

They were using this question as a trap in order to have a basis of accusing Jesus. Jesus bent down and started to write in the dust with his finger. When they kept on questioning him, he straightened up and said to them "If anyone of you is without sin, let him be the first to throw a stone at her.

Again Jesus stooped down and wrote in the dust. At this, those who heard his words, began to go away one at a time. The older ones first until Jesus was left with, only the woman standing there. Jesus straightened up and asked her

"Woman, where are they? Has no

> one condemned you?" "No one sir,"
> she said. "Then neither do I
> condemn you," Jesus declared.
> "Go now and leave your life of sin.".
> John 8: 3-11

At the end, he did not say to her. "Go away, everything is okay." His counsel was, to 'leave' her life of sin. Up to that last line, Jesus words and actions were those of grace. The final words he spoke to her, were words of truth.

John observed that Jesus managed to combine both "grace and truth", into his words and actions.

Courage

Courage, was another quality of Jesus. It was not fools courage. It was not the courage of a gladiator, although it could be said that Jesus was a 'gladiator for the truth'. What is obvious as you read different stories about Jesus, is that he was a person who had the courage to stand up for what he believed, regardless of what others thought and said.

Jesus' courage, impressed even his enemies. The teachers of the law were perhaps trying to flatter him when they said,

> "Teacher, ... You aren't swayed by
> men, because you pay no attention

to who they are." Matt 21:16

Examples of Jesus' courage include the time the woman caught in adultery was brought to him. At that time, Jesus was confronted by a hostile group of teachers and Pharisees, who were looking for a way to trap him. Instead of engaging them in an argument, cowering in fear at their words or their authority - or even retreating. Jesus paid no attention to their unreasonable demands that she be stoned, and ignored them. Jesus courage was shown by the way he bent down and began to write in the dust.

Jesus was intending to speak to this woman, but on his terms. He made the point that he did not condemn her and that all people are sinners, and after the teachers of the law had melted away then he spoke to her.

Another illustration of Jesus having the courage to do what he believed was right, was when he was in a synagogue. On this occasion, there was a man with a shriveled hand in the Synagogue and the Pharisees were watching to see if Jesus would heal the man, on the Sabbath!

Knowing well that their law prohibited such actions on the Sabbath, Jesus went ahead and did it, anyway! Jesus did not whisper to the man. "We do not want to cause a scene here in the Synagogue and upset these Pharisees. Just wait till after the service is over, and then when they are gone, in private I will pray for you." Rather he said

"Stand up in front of everyone"

so that the Pharisees could see exactly what he was doing.

Inappropriate or irrational anger, is not a Christian virtue, but it has been said that if we lack any anger, we may never act on anything, or do anything or resist anything.

A number of times Jesus was angry and there is a point here, for all of us. Jesus was never angry that he (personally) had been maligned or inconvenienced. The only time he was angry, is when man-made laws prevented him from healing or doing good.

Another example of Jesus having appropriate anger is the time he cleared the Temple of traders and money changers, who were ripping off pilgrims. It was a monopoly situation where religious requirements were used to charge pilgrims, inflated prices for their offerings and inflated prices for their money exchange.

Throughout his ministry, Jesus acted with the courage to do and say, what he believed, was right.

There were reasons for his actions

Each time Jesus acted, he cut to the heart of the matter. To the leaders who demanded that the woman be stoned, he went to the heart of the matter by addressing the issue of their own, sinfulness. "He who is without sin, may cast the first stone."

Before he healed the man with the withered arm in the Synagogue, he went to the heart of the matter by addressing the Pharisees with the question

> "Which is lawful on the Sabbath: to
> do good or to do evil, to save life or
> to kill?" John 3: 1-7

In other words, to Jesus it was appropriate to good to people any time. But especially on the Sabbath and especially in a Synagogue.

And while at the Temple, Jesus also went to the heart of the matter with the traders and money lenders when he said.

> "My house shall be called a house
> of prayer but you have made it a
> den of thieves."

A non conformist

The term 'non conformist' is a tag, sometimes given to someone who by implication, goes out of their way 'not' to conform, with the majority.

In a way, that describes Jesus, but I need to qualify that statement. John the Baptist was a real religious, non-conformist! He dressed in sheep skins. Ate a spartan diet of locusts and honey and conducted his ministry in a remote spot, well away from most citizens of Israel.

Jesus was a non-conformist also, but in a very different way to John the Baptist. He did not dress differently from other men. He did not avoid people. In fact he welcomed them and dined with them in their houses.

He was available to people in the countryside, in the towns, and in Jerusalem – the Capital city yet he was a non-conformist in a number of ways.

Jesus was a 'non conformist', not by his dress or what he ate or where he ministered to people, he was non conformist because he led a life so different to:

1. Other religious people, and

2. Virtually everyone else at the time

When I write, "Virtually every one else at the time. Who then or now, believes a person should forgive and bless their enemies? Surely the most appropriate act is to get even? Or get revenge or hold a grudge? With this teaching and so many others Jesus was so different to, most if not all people of his time.

But Jesus did not conform to the norms of a religious leader, either. As an example, the Apostle John wrote

> "Just then his disciples returned and were *surprised* to find him talking with a woman." John 4:27 (Italics added)

There were probably three reasons, John wrote that the disciples were "surprised."

Why would Jesus make a point of talking to a woman? Why not? Jesus emphasized the fact that in the beginning God had made humans both "male and female" Matt 19:4 The obvious implication of that statement is that because both males and females are made in God's image both must be of incredible worth.

Why would Jesus talk to an immoral woman? Jesus was later to say "I have come to save sinners", and this woman certainly qualified as that.

But this immoral woman, was also a Samaritan. A half breed, despised by the religious authorities.

So, why would Jesus talk to an immoral, 'Samaritan' woman? At the end of his ministry, he instructed the disciples to go into 'all' the world - to people of every race Matt 28:1.

That was why Jesus was happy to talk with this person, who happened to be immoral, a woman and a Samaritan – and it "surprised the disciples that Jesus was so different to the religious authorities who would not have talked to her for all of those reasons.

His teachings

Six times in Matthew chapter five Jesus is recorded as saying, "But I tell you". Prior to the "But I tell you", Jesus addressed the thinking of the person of the time. They thought that obeying the law meant merely doing things like not murdering – but Jesus indicated through his teaching, extended God's ways to their thoughts as well.

Another way of phrasing what Jesus said, is this: 'The norm for most of you is this….., but 'God's way is…..

The most obvious contrast to the thinking and practices of the time was how Jesus taught others to treat their enemies. People then and now have a number of options in relation to their enemies.

Level 1: Extract revenge.

Level 2: Do not extract revenge, but hold a grudge

Level 3: After a 'great' struggle, decide magnanimously to forgive their enemies.

Level 4: Forgive them without struggling over the fact.

Level 5: Forgive and pray for them.

Level 6: Forgive, pray for them, and do good to them.

It is likely that many of those listening to Jesus will have lived by an opposite scale.

Minus 1 – Do not forgive your enemies, just ignore them.

Minus 2 – Do not forgive them, and look for ways to blacken their name.

Minus 3 – Do not forgive them and seek to get even.

Minus 4 – Seek to get revenge, but on an even greater scale than that inflicted on you.*

*It is likely that most readers of this book are Christians, and may not think that Minus 4, occurs.

I can recall the comments of a man who became a Christian through an Alpha course. He said that prior to becoming a Christian, when someone double-crossed him or caused him trouble, he spent months finding as much as he could about the person who had double-crossed him, or caused him trouble.

Then, once he had learned as much as he could about that person who had double crossed him, he made a point of extracting at least 'twice' the revenge (if not more), than what had been inflicted on him.

Jesus teachings about forgiving and blessing enemies did not conform to the norms, then or now.

Nor did Jesus conform to what the disciples of teachers like John the Baptist, expected of the Messiah, so they came to Jesus to ask if he was the Messiah. Luke 7:18

Perhaps the disciples of John reasoned. John wore sheep-skins, while Jesus wore the normal clothing of a male. John's ministry was in a remote spot. Jesus ministry was in the towns and cities or the countryside near the towns. John dined on locusts and wild honey while Jesus wined and dined in the houses many different people.

He enjoyed social occasions such as weddings and shared meals. In fact he was mislabeled, a "glutton and drunkard" by critics. Matt 11:19

Jesus did not come with a desire or a need to be different from the crowd. To be different, for the sake of being different.

And in being different to the norms of both secular people and religious people, it was not because he was thick-skinned. He wept over the death of individuals like Lazarus and over the blindness of the people of Jerusalem. Matt 23:37

The reason Jesus was so different to both secular and religious people is that he was at a different place to them. He was at point (c) while they were either at point (a) or point (b)

That is illustrated by Jesus' conversation with a Samaritan woman, at Jacob's well. When Jesus spoke with her at Jacob's well, she raised the main point of dispute between the Samaritans and the Jews: the location of the true place of worship.

For Jews, the only true place of worship was (a) Jerusalem. For Samaritans, it was (b)

Samaria, but to Jesus, the correct answer was (c) neither!

Jesus told her in effect, it does not matter to God **where** you worship, as long as you worship him in Spirit and in truth. John 4:19-24 i.e. It was the 'how' and it is not the 'where' that matters to God.

In so many ways Jesus was at a different point to other people, both religious and non religious. Religious teachers thought long prayers would impress God. The average Jew thought revenge was the best way to treat your enemies. And the Samaritans and Jews had a distinctly different view about which city, was the true place of worship.

The way in which Jesus was different to most people of his time is best described by the words of the paraphrase 'The Living Bible'.

> "Don't copy the behavior and customs of this world, but be a new and different person with a fresh newness in all you do and think. Then you will learn from your own experience how his ways will really satisfy you." Rom 12.2 (L.B)

There was a fresh newness in the life and religion of Jesus, which though antagonizing some, attracted many people to his faith even some teachers of the law.

Towards the end of the Gospels and in the early chapters of the books of Acts, we read of many Pharisees and Priests becoming disciples of Jesus.

So even some of those religious leaders who are portrayed in the Gospels as being people log-jammed by their laws and rituals, saw in Jesus, something new and different in the way he served God. Something they found so attractive, that they left their well-paid and structured life for a life, far less comfortable but more rewarding life – as a disciple of Jesus.

A friend of mine is a truck driver. At one stage he was the lone Christian among a group of non-Christian truck drivers. After a period of time one of the truck drivers who appeared the toughest and 'least Christian' (i.e. you could tell that by how regularly he used the of"F... , in his language), came up to my friend and said. "You are a Christian". To which my friend replied, "I am".

"No", said the non-Christian driver "I mean, you are a, real Christian!"

There was a fresh newness. An attractive difference about my friends life, and this non-

Christian man, had noticed it.

Chapter 3

The King of Love

The words of a hymn are,

> The King of Love my shepherd is…

Though most countries do not have a king or queen, the word king or queen still symbolizes the ultimate position for any male or female. And the words, Prince and Princess still hold a powerful significance.

Some businesses include the word '**king**' in their business name to represent the idea that they have the ultimate product or service in their field.

By reviewing the three years of his ministry, Jesus richly deserved the title 'The King of Love' .

When Jesus was asked, which is the greatest commandment, he quickly replied by quoting the first commandment which includes the words, "to love God." However at that time, Jesus added another commandment. One not found in the Ten Commandments.

The new commandment Jesus added, was a Jesus original,

> "You shall love your neighbor as yourself." Matt 22:38 NLT

Then Jesus followed up that answer with this comment.

> "All law and prophets hang on these two commandments." Matt 22:40 NIV

A way of rephrasing those words of Jesus, is this:

> "Our whole religion can be compressed down into these two, simple commands."

'**Love**' is at the heart of the new covenant religion Jesus founded. Aware that he was soon going to be leaving this Earth and returning to heaven, Jesus took the twelve disciples aside for a special teaching session, in which he taught key teachings that would frame the beliefs and actions of the new Church once he was gone.

During that foundational teaching session, among the key teachings, were a series of love relationships. He said

> "As the Father has loved me, so I have loved you."

and,

> "Love each other." John 15:9&12 NIV

Note, Jesus used the word "love", for three different relationships. The relationship between himself and God his Father. Between himself and his disciples, and between, each other.

Jesus loved people, because he came from love. He came from God, and God is love. And, not coincidentally a fruit of the Spirit is love. In a few words, when Jesus came to this Earth, he did not stumble onto that love was going to be the durable quality for human an divine relationships. He viewed love as the only basis for human and divine relationships.

But what does that mean at a practical level? Love is the starting point, but it's outworking is as varied as the stars in the sky.

Sometimes love means being patient. And Jesus had to be patient with the first disciples as they argued over who would be the greatest and deserted Jesus when the High Priest's soldiers arrived.

Sometimes love is believing the best of people, despite their failings. When Jesus saw his disciples sleeping in the garden of Gethsemane, before his arrest. He would have been tempted to ditch them and start with a new group because they were sleeping when he needed their prayer support most. Love believes the best.

But what is love? Love is first of all an attitude. So what were Jesus attitudes? It appears that a number of attitudes motivated Jesus.

That God loves all people regardless of their race or gender, or whether they were well or sick, poor or rich.

Love is expressed by both words and actions and by words. Actions such as healing, helping, hugging and holding and giving Facilitating and planning, good for others.

Love   is   expressed   by   words   of

encouragement, and faith and forgiveness and truth. Jesus selected words that honored people.

After Zacchaeus repented of his cheating life-style, Jesus called him "a son of Abraham." There is no greater compliment you can pay a Jewish person than to call them a son or daughter of Abraham.

On another occasion, Jesus spoke to the disciples about the actions of a woman who had poured expensive perfume on his head. He said

> "She has done a beautiful thing to me." Matt 26:10

Judas was right. The money she spent on that perfume, could have been given to the poor but Jesus recognized that she had pushed past the outer ring of invited guests and did what to her, was something she wanted to do for Jesus.

To Jesus, loving others, was not complex once a love attitude has been adopted. The Pharisees and teachers of the law had a complex system by which what could be done for others was measured and to whom it was go be given was described. Certain groups were in, and certain groups were out.

Jesus dispensed with those regulations of who, and how much in favor of a simple principle. "Do to others, what you would have them do for you." Matt 7:12

Once that principle is inscribed in a persons heart and mind then good can be done to any person, any time, any where. There is no need for a manual to describe and quantify what love is, For to the person who has this love-attitude in their heart, and applies this love principle to the people they meet in life.

John Wesley came up with a saying that goes something like this. This saying amplifies that principle, Jesus taught.

Do all the good you can. As often as you can. Where ever you can. To whoever you can.

It is appropriate that what we say, reflects love. That our actions, reflect love but sometimes love doesn't have to be something particular we do or say. Just enjoying the company of others, is also an act of love, because it shows we accept the other person, for who they are.

Jesus was a regular visitor to the house of Mary, Martha and Lazarus, where he enjoyed their hospitality and company.

How Jesus came to be a regular guest at their

house is an interesting question, for Luke tells us that disciples like Joanna and Mary Magdalene, became disciples of Jesus because he had either healed them. Or set them free from demons – and out of gratitude they followed Jesus, and the other disciples from village to village and contributed to their costs from their own money. Luke 8:1-3 But what about Mary and Martha?

We are not told that they were healed of any sickness or set free from demons. So how was it, that out of the hundreds and sometimes thousands who crowded around Jesus, Mary and Martha got past the crowds and the twelve.

We do not know the answer to that question, but somehow they did and got close enough to say something like this.

"Rabbi. Whenever you are traveling from Galilee to Jerusalem and need somewhere to stay, or even a meal. You are welcome to stay in our house in Bethany." (which is not far from Jerusalem)

Somehow they got past the crowds and the twelve, and Jesus accepted their offer on a regular basis.

When he did come to their home, the Gospel

writers do not tell us that Jesus healed any of them, so Jesus visits were based on friendship and love. John tells us

> "Jesus loved Martha and her sister and Lazarus." John 11:5

Near the end of his ministry, Jesus called Lazarus, a "friend." John 11:11

Jesus knew that real love, is not just temporary emotion. Love has to involve our feelings, but it is springs from what is in heart and the values that reside there. As Jesus astutely recognized "Out of the heart, the mouth speaks."

Jesus made love a commandment. In fact, it was the only commandment Jesus made. That commandment was

> "My command is this: Love one another as I have loved you." John 4:34

Jesus knew that feelings can pass, but a commitment to love, is what sustains any relationship through thick and thin.

It was when Lazarus died, that Jesus' love for him, became compassion.

Compassion
Compassion is a branch of love. Compassion

is something a person feels and shows when they have become aware that someone has is hurting or suffered a loss. Particularly something they are helpless to do, anything about. The disciples of Jesus, noticed that he was frequently moved by compassion for those who were helpless.

Isaiah prophesied about that a compassion, would be part of Jesus' nature. Isaiah wrote

> "a bruised reed he will not break."
> Isa 42:3

Jesus' ministry as he went around the villages and towns of Israel was to all, but Jesus could not help but notice the 'bruised and bent reeds' among the people. When Jesus heard that the only son of a widow had died, instantly he felt compassion for her.

She had lost her husband and virtually the only means of income, and now she had lost her only son. Luke 7:11-17 That loss was first and foremost personal. To lose her husband and a son is a double-blow, no woman wants.

But there was an added burden on her shoulders by these losses. Unless her husband had investments, this woman would have become virtually destitute, and Jesus would have known that.

The type of predicament this widow faced is hinted at in the Old Testament story of Naomi. Elimalech, husband of Naomi, died. Ruth 1:3 Following his death, her daughter-in-law Ruth went to the barley fields to follow behind those harvesting, so she could pick up any husks that had been missed by those picking the barley. She did that simply, so she and Naomi could eat. Ruth 2:2

For Naomi and Ruth and other women in those times, there was seldom any other choice. There was no such thing as life Insurances. No Government support for widows, and few jobs a women could do outside of the home. Factories, offices and companies are more recent inventions.

Knowing the economic future faced her. Knowing she had been bruised by the loss of her husband and then bent by the loss of her only son. Luke wrote:

> "his heart went out to her," Luke 7:13

Jesus knew the score.

1. Tragedy one: The loss of her of husband.

2. Tragedy two: The loss of her only son.

3. Tragedy three: The loss of income.

4. Tragedy four: The loss of status and standing before the law.

Another occasion, Jesus compassion quickly came to the surface. This occasion was when a man with leprosy came to Jesus and begged him on his knees, to make him clean. In the Gospel of Mark, we read:

> "Filled with compassion, Jesus reached out his hand and touched the man. "I am willing," he said." Mark 1:40 & 41

The significance of the words the leper used at that time, were not lost on Jesus because he understood the reason for them. The leper did not come to Jesus and say, "please make me well", though, that is what he wanted. He wanted to be made well. But this leper said to Jesus, "make me clean".

The words the leper, used were a reflection of society in those times. Once it became obvious a person had contracted leprosy, it did not matter whether the person was the mayor of the town. A successful business person. A sports star, or whoever you were.

As soon as it became obvious that a person had leprosy, that person had to leave their family and friends immediately, and join that untouchable class of people called lepers, and live in exile, well away from the rest of society.

And whenever someone got near a leper, the leper was supposed to call out loudly – "unclean, unclean!" So it must have seemed to the person who had leprosy and been forced to leave their home, that their name was no longer Zacharias or Johanna or… but their new name was now "Unclean"

And they had to live in a colony of people who had exactly the same name, "Unclean."

It was because Jesus knew the reason this man used the word "unclean", that he had compassion for him.

Most Christians today, will not meet people like that leper who knelt in front of Jesus, because leper colonies today, only exist in a limited number of countries.

However the challenge for us today is to put on the same type of glasses that Jesus wore. (figuratively speaking) when he met the leper.

Jesus wore glasses, and by looking through those glasses, everybody he saw was, somebody God loved.

Jesus compassion included those who were

side-lined by incurable diseases, but extended to everyone in society. People with, any type of burden.

He said

> "Come to me, 'all' you who are weary and burdened, and I will give you rest!" Matt 11:28

Jesus recognized that people can have all sorts of burdens. For some, the burden is a family member is not whole - physically, emotionally, mentally or spiritually. Some people are burdened by financial problems or the loss of a family member or job. Some are burdened because someone close is addicted to something.

But Jesus' compassion went wider than that. He felt compassion, not only for individuals, but entire groups of people.

> "When Jesus landed and saw a large crowd, he had compassion on them because they were like sheep without a shepherd." Mark 6:34

Jesus had compassion on this crowd because they had no direction.

Another time Jesus had compassion for the city of Jerusalem for a similar reason. He said in anguish

> "O Jerusalem, Jerusalem, you who kill the prophets and stone those sent to you, how often have I longed to gather your children together, as a hen gathers her chicks under her wings, but you were not willing." Matt 23:37

Jerusalem is a city on an elevated site but above it is the Mount of Olives, and it is possible to stand on the Mount of Olives, and look down on the city take it in – all in one sweep.

So perhaps it was when Jesus viewed Jerusalem from the Mount of Olives that he spoke those anguished words.

Jesus had different types of compassion. Compassion for those whose life had taken a turn so that they were bent or marginalized like the leper. But Jesus also had compassion on people and nations.

People who are asking whether salvation is to be found in a political party or philosophy or religious movement or success or in worshiping nature or.......

Goals that seem to promise salvation but which are in themselves empty containers – for salvation is to be found in one person alone. That is Jesus.

So who did Jesus love?

The Apostle Paul wrote

> "There is neither Jew nor Greek,
> slave nor free, male nor female, for
> you are all one in Christ Jesus."
> Gal 3:28

These words summarize Jesus' thinking. He did not love people according to race or position or gender. In fact the categories of people he loved is wider than Paul wrote about. If I could add to those words the Apostle wrote, they would also include the young and old, the sick and possessed. The poor and the wealthy. Absolutely, everyone.

Nicodemus who came to him with a question (John 3:1), was a Pharisee, and because of the system of religious taxes, Pharisees and other religious leaders soon became wealthy.

Along with wealth, they had power. Power to detain, and arrest people. The fact that we read about this private conversation between Nicodemus and Jesus, implies Nicodemus became a life-long disciple of Jesus. Jesus loved such people.

Grace

Compassion is a branch of love, and so is grace. The word grace means, undeserved or unmerited love. It was the Apostle Paul who introduced the doctrine of grace, but it was Jesus who demonstrated (by the spade-load) what grace meant, thought his words and actions towards two people.

Two examples that stand out in the Gospels are Jesus' words and actions towards the woman caught in adultery and Jesus' words and actions towards Peter - after Peter had denied Jesus, three times.

Jesus gave Peter undeserved love, by graciously asking him three times "Do you love me?" Most would have thought it appropriate for Jesus to poor scorn on Peter, for being afraid of the words of a servant girl (before his trial) or it would have been appropriate if Jesus had simply ignored Peter, or calling him, "a failure" or "a coward."

However, Jesus graciously chose to remind Peter of the three times he had denied Jesus by asking him three times, "Do you love me?"

If that was all that Jesus said at that time, it would have been an example of amazing grace! But each time that Peter responded to Jesus' question, Jesus said to Peter. "Feed my Lambs" or "Feed my sheep."

This was, 'grace (undeserved love) upon

grace. (more undeserved love!) Jesus was in effect saying to Peter. Even though you denied that you knew me (not very long ago), now I am not only forgiving you. I am asking you to be 'the' leader of the new Church. To feed the lambs (the new converts), and the sheep. Those who are already my disciples.

If Jesus did not demonstrate that grace towards Peter, the book of Acts would be very different. After the coming of the Holy Spirit early in the book of Acts it likely to have have moved on from there to chapter nine, with the ministry of Paul.

The early church began after Jesus ascended to heaven, because of two factors. The coming of the Holy Spirit in power, and the leadership of Peter. The forgiven one. The man who was shown, grace upon grace, responded to that grace, by leading the early Church, as Jesus asked him to.

Jesus also told parables that included examples of grace upon grace. The parables of the good Samaritan and prodigal son, are the two notable examples of parables which include, grace upon grace.

Those listening to the parable of the good Samaritan, would have known of the prejudice that existed between the Jews and

Samaritans, so as they followed the story, they would 'not' expected, in the parable or story that Jesus told for the Samaritan to stop for the Jew, beaten up and lying beside the road.

They would would have understood* if, in the parable Jesus had said. "The Samaritan passed by and said. "That serves you right – you wretched Jew."

*The Pharisees had a prayer. "May my eyes never set on a Samaritan."

Instead of what they expected, in the parable, the Samaritan stopped and bandaged the wounds of the Jew and put him on his own donkey and took him to the safety of an Inn.

If the Samaritan had done that alone, most Jews would have been dumbfounded at this extraordinary example of grace. But in the parable, the Samaritan went further, and showed grace upon grace. He paid for the accommodation of the Jewish man and promised to come back and pay more, if that was necessary.

There is another extraordinary example of grace in Jesus' teaching. In another parable Jesus told, a son who demanded his share of the estate left home, and spent the money on parties and prostitutes.

In doing so, he had by the standards of those times, 'ruined' both his father's and his family's name. Something that would have been a much greater sin than mis-spending his inheritance in the culture of those times.

Because of the son's actions, if the father had decided to have nothing with this son, ever again, most of those listening would have understood. But in the story (or parable) Jesus told, as soon as the father saw the son, he 'ran' towards him, hugged him and put a ring on his finger. The father threw a cloak around him, and threw a party.

Most of those listening to the parable, would have expected, at the point where Jesus described the reappearance of the son, that the fathers reaction would have been, one of the following:

- Turned away in disgust.

- Angrily rejecting the son.

- Showing, cold indifference.

- Or perhaps, in a magnanimous act, demonstrated a sullen acceptance, at the son's return.

Instead, and by an extraordinary twist of

grace, the father came running to meet the son, and threw a welcoming party.

Can you see the connection? Grace upon grace is a chandelier that shines in both Jesus teachings, and in his words and actions towards people.

In the ministry of Jesus, there was grace upon grace towards Peter, and the woman caught in adultery. Grace towards Zacchaeus and grace towards Mary Magdalene Grace towards Thomas the doubter, and forgiving grace towards, those who crucified him.

Chapter 4

Understanding Jesus and understanding the Teachings of Jesus

The teachings of Jesus is a huge* subject, and requires a separate book, to do them justice so in this chapter there will not be anything like a complete review of all his teachings. Instead, the focus will be on the 'key' to unlocking and understanding, most of Jesus' teachings.

*One Bible scholar analyzed every thing Jesus said and concluded that Jesus taught 300 different subjects.

A quick overview of his teachings.

His teachings are found in four Gospels each of whose writers had a different slant. There are three principle methods Jesus got his message across. By teaching. By asking questions or at least. Inviting listeners to ask questions about their beliefs and life-styles and through parables.

Jesus told 32 parables which are stories with a meaning. His teachings are gathered in two principle blocks. Matthew chapters 5-7 and John chapters 15-17. In those blocks of teachings, Jesus set out to inform his disciples what they would need to know once he was gone. As such, both blocks of teaching are very significant.

However, equally significant are what I call, 'the spontaneous teachings'. These 'spontaneous teachings', were usually answers to questions people him asked him while he was in the street or Synagogue or wherever people met him.

Some of Jesus' 'spontaneous teachings' came about because of an unexpected situation, such as the time when the disciples had been arguing who was the greatest in the kingdom. Jesus seized that opportunity to tell the disciples that those who wanted to be great must be, "the servant of all." Mark 9:35

Other examples of 'spontaneous teachings', include:

"the first and greatest commandment is. Love the Lord your God with all your heart and with all your soul and with all your mind. ... And the second is like it. You shall love your neighbor as yourself. All the Law and the Prophets hang of these two commandments. Matt 22:40

We only have these words of Jesus because Pharisees came up to Jesus and asked him. "Which are the most important commandments?"

Another example of 'spontaneous teachings', is this one. The Pharisees and Herodians came up to Jesus and tried to trap him into saying something they could arrest him for. They asked. "Is it right to pay taxes to Caesar or not?" Matt 22:17

Jesus reply was.

..."give to Caesar what belongs to Caesar, and give to God, what belongs to God." Matt 22:21 NLT

Some of the most valuable sayings and

teachings of Jesus, because of spontaneous encounters that arose.

The kingdom of God

After Jesus returned from his time of testing in the desert, he began his ministry proclaiming.

"Repent for the kingdom of heaven in near." Matt 4:17 NIV

Occasionally Jesus talked about the "Church", but mainly he spoke about the kingdom of God or kingdom of heaven. For readers not sure what the distinction is between the Church, and the kingdom of God, I will explain.

There is your local Church and then there is the Church universal which includes every Christian Church and every Christian organization and there then is the kingdom of God.

The kingdom of God includes every Church that preaches the Gospel and every Christian organization but the kingdom is not confined to any building of any Church or Christian organization It is where, God's people are. That is anywhere. Everywhere all 1.8 billion Christians are.

That means the kingdom of God is at our local Church, and every local Church on the face of the Earth. And at our home or work.

And with Christians at the beach, or by a river. Or on the mission field, or in their business. Or at a conference or in a counseling room. Or in the class-room.

Wherever God's people are, the kingdom of God is there. That is what Jesus meant when he said...."nor will people say, Here it I, There it is, because the kingdom of God is within you." Luke 17:21 NIV

Altitude in the kingdom of God.

There is a saying, 'our attitude determines our altitude'. That is so true in the kingdom of God.

Our altitude in the kingdom of God, is determined by our altitude.

If anyone understands Jesus, and understands Jesus teachings, it is because they understand the significance he placed on attitude.

A friend told me this story, which is relevant to this chapter. He was talking to a Professor from a prominent university in England and the Professor said. "I do not value staff in my department for their intelligence or qualifications but for their attitude.

When I am interviewing people to be employed in my department at this university the person I favor is not necessarily the person with the highest qualifications or the highest IQ. The person I choose from all the suitable applicants, is the person who has the best attitude.

I have learned that a person with the best attitude to his or her work (but who may have lesser qualifications and IQ than others applying for the job), will contribute more to my department."

This Professor also pointed out. "If you give each letter of the alphabet a numerical value in sequential order with A = 1, B = 2, C = 3 and Z = 26. The numerical values of the word, attitude, add up to 100. I.e. 100%"

Now there is a sense in which Jesus, and this Professor are on the same wave-length. Jesus would like to employ people in his kingdom. People who have the right attitude. His attitudes.

Attitude is such a factor in Jesus' teachings, it would be appropriate to call Jesus:

the king of attitude.

Jesus did not mention the word attitude during the course of his teachings but, as hopefully the rest of this chapter will demonstrate having a Jesus-like attitude is so important for the kingdom of God.

In virtually all the parables Jesus told, the reason he told these parables, was to get people listening to , ask questions about their attitude.

Probably the best known teachings of Jesus, are those found in Matthew chapters 5-7. Among those teachings are ten sayings that have come to be called 'the beatitudes'. And as that title suggests, the beatitudes are full of attitude.

The beatitudes are significant, for a number of reasons. Some suggest they are Jesus' version, of the ten commandments. If that is an accurate conclusion, what Jesus (the king of attitude) has done, is this.

He has taken the ten commandments, and repackaged them with a new attitude. With the new packaging, the same ten commandments are changed from, from thou shalt not, to, thou shalt!

Changed from, do not to, do – by inviting those listening to him to 'desire' righteousness or as Jesus said. "Hunger and thirst for righteousness."

A person who hungers and thirsts for righteousness, is not going to steal and lie and murder because they have an attitude. I want to do what is right, for my neighbor

The rest of the beatitudes continue in the same way. In the beatitudes he encouraged listeners to desire to be humble. To desire justice and to be merciful and for a pure n heart. And to work for peace, to do what is right, as followers of Jesus.

The word beatitude, is a combination of two words, 'be' and 'attitude'. To paraphrase that word, Jesus was essentially saying. This is what I would like your attitudes to be.

By beginning each beatitude with the word "Blessed", Jesus was dangling an incentive in front of the people listening to him. He was, in effect asking this question.

Do you want to live a life with God's favor on it – for that is what someone has who is blessed by God. They have his favor. If so, I recommend you live with these attitudes to:

> "the poor in Spirit", "those who mourn" "being meek", "righteousness", "mercy", purity, being a "peacemaker", "righteousness".

Apart from the Beatitudes, 'attitude' infuses virtually every teaching of Jesus. In his teachings, we discover Jesus attitude to God, to the Holy Spirit, to worship, to miracles, to freedom, to money, to possessions, to the talents we have, to sick people, to sinful people, to people of other races, to religion and to life.

His attitudes were 'so' different to the attitudes people expected of a religious teacher, that people were either: attracted to Jesus or repelled by him. What was attractive, was his attitudes.

In his teachings we find Jesus' attitude to money, to giving and receiving, to possessions and to life itself. To leadership. To spiritual authority. To position in the kingdom of God. To promotion in the kingdom of God, and to pay in the kingdom.

We find in his teachings, his attitude to our gifts and others gifts. Attitudes to spiritual authority. To worship, to prayer. To sinners. To sin. To suffering.

Jesus words and teachings are infused with attitude. Teachings he wanted his disciples to:

- remember Matt 28:20

- understand Matt 13:16

- put into practice Matt 7:24

"Do you not understand?" Was a question Jesus asked the first disciples. And in various teachings, Jesus made the point to his disciples. I don't want you just to listen to my teachings, but to understand what I am saying and the attitude that is behind them.

Jesus also recognized that the greatest teachings in the world, are of little use unless disciples put them into practice. So he said. "Therefore everyone who hears these words of mine and puts them into practice is like a wise man who built his house on a rock." Matt 7:24

Jesus wanted his disciple to remember what he taught, for among his final instructions (often called the great commission), are these words.

"Teach these new disciples to obey *all* the commands I have given you." Matt 28:20 NLT (italics added for emphasis)

An extraordinary example of attitude – in Jesus teachings

The Roman soldiers made it a practice that they while on a march, they could ask any citizen of the empire, to carry their pack a mile. It is certain that most complied, but it is easy to imagine that most complied, with great resentment.

Jesus taught his disciples to comply to this request, but with a very different attitude. Imagine the following scene.

Citizen *A* is asked to carry the pack of a Roman soldier for a mile – and when he does so, walks every step of that mile with resentment and under his or her breath, is wishing the Roman soldier harm.

And even after Citizen A has returned the pack, for the rest of their day, there is a bitter taste in their mind and spirit in which Citizen A goes over the injustice. "Today, I had to carry a Roman soldiers pack, for a mile!"

Citizen *B* by contrast, receives exactly the same request, but instead of walking each step of that mile with resentment - sings hymns and smiles at the Roman soldier. And then, when the mile is up and the soldier is expecting to have his pack returned in a hurry, Citizen *B* smiles and says. "Look, it will save me going to the gym today, I will take your pack an extra mile!"

In contrast to Citizen *A*, Citizen *B* goes home that night, with a light spirit. He or she is learning that sometimes, losing is winning –

an attitude that Jesus wanted to foster in his disciples.

Following on are other teachings of Jesus which demonstrate that attitude is, everything to Jesus.

Attitude to sin

Like many people today, some people in his time pretended sin no longer mattered. Jesus had a different attitude. "Go now, and leave your life of sin." John 8:11

Sinning isn't winning

The reason people today discard/disregard moral laws, is that they believe by discarding them, they will find freedom. Jesus recognized that attitude in the people of his time, and had a different attitude. His attitude was. The core of the law still applies and by ignoring or discarding that core instead of finding freedom - a person becomes a slave to sin or their passions. John 8:34

Attitudes to wrong-doing Luke 23:39-43

One criminals attitude was. I do not care about the Romans who put me on this cross. I do not care about those I have harmed or killed. I do not care about God or Jesus. His attitude was simply. Jesus if you can, just get me off this cross.

That attitude compared with the other criminal who cared about the wrong he had done, what God would say once he came before God, in judgment

Attitude to repentance

Throughout his ministry placed a high value on genuine repentance. He began his teaching ministry saying, "Repent." In a parable Jesus told, the son who had misspent his inheritance, genuinely repented. When he did so, he was given an amazing welcome.

Jesus would be consistent with that value throughout his ministry. Cheating Zacchaeus, repented and did a U-turn, so Jesus exclaimed. "Salvation has come to this house today." With the repentant thief on the cross, Jesus said. "Today you will be in paradise with me."

An attitude to sinfulness

Jesus told the Pharisees who were suggesting that a woman caught in adultery be stoned. "He who is without sin, may cast the first stone."

Jesus attitude was. Before throwing stones at the sinfulness of others, first remind yourself that we are, all sinners. Further, Jesus was aware of God's attitude to the wicked.

"He causes his sun to rise on the evil and the

good." Matt 5:45

Attitude towards love

For Jesus, love was the most vital ingredient, in every relationship, including our relationship with ourselves. When asked which were the greatest commandments, his reply was to love God, our neighbor and ourselves.

During his pre-trial teaching sessions, Jesus spoke about a number of love relationships. These are recorded in John's Gospel.

I love my Father. 14:31

God loves me. 15:9

I love you 15:9

Remain in my love 15: 9

Your love for me, is shown by obeying my teachings 15:10

Loving your fellow Christians is so important, I have made it a command 15:12 .See also 17

Love is shown, not by getting, but if necessary - laying down your life. 15:13

Attitude to the past/present and future

"So do not worry about tomorrow it will have enough worries of it's own." Matt 6:34 GN Implicit in Jesus' words, are these attitudes

- You and I cannot change anything

about tomorrow, by worrying about it
today.

- We will probably ruin today, by worrying
about tomorrow.

- God knows about your tomorrow and
will take care of anything that occurs
tomorrow, 'if only' we will put tomorrow
in his hands and concentrate on today.

Attitude towards the past

"He who plows and looks back, is not worthy
of the kingdom." Luke 9:62

It is implicit in these words of Jesus that he
wants us to be concerned about two things -
the present and the future. Not about the past,
whether there was success or failure. There
can be lessons from the past but Jesus wants
those who plow the soil, in each generation to
focus on the present, and the future.

In saying this, Jesus was on the same track
as Isaiah before him and Paul, after him. The
Apostle wrote... "Forgetting what is behind,
and straining towards what is ahead, I press
on." Phil 3:13 And Isaiah, "Forget the former
things do not dwell on the past. See I am
doing a new thing! Isa 43:18

God's attitude to what we need

Jesus indicated God's attitude tow what we
need. Ask and you will receive. Even though

God knows our needs, he still wants us to ask in faith. If God just gave us everything we need, without us even asking we would live life with an attitude.

I can spend money on what I like because God is going to see me right – and we would never anything we had, or life itself.

Attitude towards money Matt 6:19-21

Jesus attitude was. True riches, are riches in heaven, and not on Earth. In Jesus' words, our riches are where, our heart is.

Jesus identified the "love of money" as the problem for humans – not having money or earning, , significant amounts of money.

See also, 1 Tim 6:10

Attitude towards the Kingdom of God.

Instead, be concerned above everything else with the kingdom of God and with what he requires of you, and he will provide you with all these other things. Matt 6:33 GN

Value of the kingdom

The kingdom of God is like finding hidden treasure or a pearl of enormous value. Matt 13:44-45

Count the cost before entering the kingdom Luke 9:25-33

The essence of this parable is. Before you try

to enter the kingdom, count the cost in the same way someone going on a trip or building a house would consider the cost, before doing either.

And there were reasons Jesus asked his disciples to count the cost, before entering the kingdom. In another parable, the parable of the sower, Jesus painted a picture of people who would leave the kingdom, for four reasons:

- They have not understood the incredible worth of being a child of God.

- When trouble or difficulty comes, they think. We only want a religion where we get blessed, so we are out of here.

- Another leaves because, gradually, getting busy with life leads to becoming too busy for God.

- Then there are those who find the attractions of financial success in this life, so rewarding, that the gloss eternal wealth and the privilege of belonging to the kingdom of God, loses it's appeal.

    Matt 13:18-21

In the verses above, Jesus is simply saying, before you become my disciple, consider whether you are prepared to pay the cost so that you don't fall by the wayside, for any of the above reasons.

Attitude to service in the kingdom of God

The parable of the talents and the parable of the workers in the vineyard, are all about attitude Jesus intentionally told these parables to get his disciples to think about their attitudes. Matt 25:1-30 & Matt 20:1-16

These parables about two, apparently, unfair situations.

(a) In the first, the parable of the talents, different people are given different amounts of talents. Some, more than others.

What that means is this. In the kingdom, some are going to be called to be: leaders in Churches and Christian organizations And some, highly recognized singers/musicians and authors.

And in secular society, some Christians are going to become highly recognized CEO's, business people, sports people, politicians, Government employees, actors, musicians and the like.

Now it could be considered unfair that God would favor a limited number of Christians with positions of power and influence and wealth and status, but, - we are talking about the kingdom of God.

And in that kingdom Jesus said. ..everyone who has, more will be given. Luke 19:26 It is implied in the parable that those who are given more, will be held more responsible for the greater number of talents they have been given.

(b) In the second parable, about the workers in the vineyard, it is unfair if those who started later are given the same pay as those who started earlier.

But that is a parable Jesus told, because he wanted those who started later, to examine their attitudes. Essentially Jesus was asking. Does it matter what pay others get as long as you get, what I agreed to pay.

It was a disciples attitude, that Jesus was testing, by telling this parable.

(c) Then there is kingdom value. In the kingdom of God, even a cup of cold water is of great worth. Jesus used a cup of cold water as an example because in Israel, for seven months of the year, it does not rain. So a cup of cold water given to a hot and thirsty person during that time would have been much appreciated. Mark 9:41

However, a cup of water, was only an

example. It is the principle that is important. That example means, in God's economy or the kingdom economy, any act or words done for the benefit of others or the kingdom is of great significance and eternal worth.

(d) Then there is the attitude of advancement in the kingdom of God. Jesus said, the pagans "lord it over those under them. But it shall not be so with you."

Whoever is great among you must be your servant. Mark 10:43

(e) Then there is our attitude to the promotion of other Christians. Peter became concerned that another disciple might be getting preferential treatment from Jesus. Jesus reply was essentially. Don't worry about the plans I have for any other Christian. Just concentrate on what I have called you to do. John 21:20-23

(f) Then there is the attitude to spiritual power and authority, in the kingdom of God. When Jesus sent the disciples out on a trial, missionary trip he gave them authority over demons and the ability to heal the sick. When he sent them out, he said.

"Freely you have received, freely give." Matt 10:8

In other words, Jesus was saying to the disciples. You did not buy this power or earn the right to see people healed and set free from demons, because you: attended the synagogue regularly or prayed regularly. You did nothing to earn it, or merit it or buy it. So because you received if freely - give freely!

From these examples, can you see that 'altitude' in the kingdom of God, is gained by adopting Jesus or Kingdom attitudes?

The World

(a) I want you to be in the World, but not of the world. John 17:15

(b) In the world, I want you to be smart.

The the people of this world are more shrewd in dealing with their own kind than are the people of light. Luke 16:8 NIV

In the New Living Translation, the follow up words, are these. "Here's the lesson. Use your worldly resources to benefit others and make friends. Then when your worldly resources are gone, they will welcome you to an eternal home." Luke 16:9

(c) In the world, I want you to be both wise – and harmless. Matt 10:16 On another occasion Jesus said, "do not cast pearls before swine" meaning. Be wise with who you entrust the truths of the kingdom.

(d) In the world contribute love and truth and grace and understanding. Jesus example John 1:14. If you do, you will be like.

- Flavor is to bland food. Matt 5:13

- Like lights in dark places. Matt 5:14

(e) Don't let the worlds opposition, deter you because I have overcome, the world. John 16:33

Jesus appreciated people with attitude

A woman with a seemingly incurable condition said to herself. "If I only touch his cloak, I will get well." Matt 9:21 GN To touch Jesus, meant pushing past the disciples and the surrounding crowd - but this woman of faith, was determined to touch Jesus garment.

The reason Jesus did not ditch Peter, even after Peter had denied Jesus three times, is that Jesus recognized Peter was also person with faith and attitude! i.e. After Jesus came walking on water and then calmed a storm. Peter thought, 'if Jesus can do, it then I must be able to do it'.

After that Peter asked Jesus if he could get out of the boat and Peter did so and then started to walking on the water, towards Jesus. We know Peter took his eyes off

Jesus, and began to sink, but I am sure, Jesus liked both Peter's insight, and his, can-do attitude and his willingness to try.

By contrast to Peter, the other disciples were still gripping the sides of the boat for safety.

Jesus attitude to gratitude.

"Were not all ten cleansed. Where are the other nine? .... Jesus said to the man who had returned to thank and had fallen down in front of him. "Rise and go your faith has made you well." Luke 17:11-19 NIV

Jesus encouraged an attitude towards faith

Our faith might be as small as a mustard seed, but exercise it. Matt 17:20

Jesus encouraged a, faith-attitude

Jesus encouraged his disciples to consider any problem they had, no matter how large it was, from God's perspective. So even if the problem was as big as a mountain, it could be moved. Matt 17:20. .

Jesus commended anyone with a great faith-attitude

When a centurion sent a servant to ask Jesus to pray for his sick servant, but not bother actually coming to his house. Jesus commended that centurion saying.

"I have not found such great faith even in Israel." Luke 7:3 NIV

An attitude of compassion, faith and humility

Jesus said, "I tell you the truth, I have not found such faith, even in Israel." Luke 7:9 NIV

The person Jesus paid this compliment to, was a Roman centurion who asked Jesus to come and pray for his sick servant. Luke 7:1-11

I believe Jesus appreciated three attitudes, implicit in this story.

(a) The Roman centurion cared about his Jewish servant, enough to want Jesus to come and pray for him.

(b) This centurion did not consider himself worthy of having Jesus come to his house

(c) Before Jesus got to his house, he sent Jesus a message. "But say the word and my servant will be healed." Luke 7:8 NIV

Attitude to giving

A poor widow put in two copper coins. Today their value would be about the same as a cent. Jesus said that she had put more money into the Temple treasury, than those who had given large gifts of money. In fact she had put in much less, than those who had given large gifts of money – but Jesus was making the point that as a percentage of her income it was many times greater.

Further, many of those giving, gave what was spare but she gave what she had to live off, trusting God to provide the rest.

Luke 21:1-3

Common values in kingdom attitudes
Can you see the pattern in Jesus' attitudes, towards small things?

- If you only have small faith, exercise it.

- If you only have small gift (even as seemingly insignificant as a cup of cold water) – still give it because even a small act of thoughtfulness like that, is of enormous value and significance, in the kingdom of God

- If you only have one talent – still use it.

The attitudes of the Pharisees
Jesus took the Pharisees and teachers of the law to task, for their attitudes. Some would tithe smallest amount of herbs, yet neglect the much more important matters like justice and mercy.

They would give, fast and pray so that *people*

would notice whereas Jesus wanted his disciples to do exactly the same things, except. He wanted his disciples to do these things, so that only *God* would notice.

The contrasts between the disciples attitudes and those of the Pharisees, is demonstrated by the way Jesus talked to an immoral Samaritan woman at a well. At that time, even the disciples (Apostles-in-the-making) were surprised.

The teachers of the law would not have stopped to talk to her because she was a woman, a Samaritan and immoral. Jesus by contrast considered those three categories perfect reasons to talk to her.

God created both male and female, so both genders were, very important in Jesus' eyes. Before he left this Earth, Jesus commanded his disciples to be witnesses in Judea, Samaria and to the ends of the Earth. Acts 1:8

This command indicates Jesus regarded people of every race is why he was happy to talk to this Samaritan woman. The third reason Jesus was happy to talk with this woman is that he said he had come to call sinners, and not the righteous. And this woman living with the sixth man, qualified as a sinner.

So from Jesus perspective, there were three, very good reasons to talk to this person at the well. She ticked all the boxes of people he wanted to meet and of people he wanted in the kingdom of God, while for the Pharisees, they were all reasons to avoid her.

Self-centered or selfish attitudes – in the disciples

There was a world of difference between the Jesus attitudes and those of the Pharisees. However, his disciples were not perfect either. They were, Apostles-in-the-making. Disciples on a journey to becoming Apostles, and Jesus had to address, some of their attitudes.

They brushed aside mothers who wanted Jesus to bless their children as if mothers and children were not of, incredible importance. Matt 19:13-15

Another time they had an argument about who would be the greatest in the kingdom of heaven. An attitude of, I am sure I will be asked to sit next to Jesus and God in heaven and consequently The angels and those people who make it to heaven, will give me honor Luke 9:49-50 Another time, James and John requested special places either side of Jesus, in heaven. Mark 10:35-40

Another time the disciples saw a person driving out demons in the name of Jesus, and the disciples tried to stop the man because, quote. .."he is not one of us."

Jesus was onto their attitude, straight away which was. This man was not "one of us" - the in-crowd. Jesus attitude was. It did not matter whether a person was part of the 12 or 70, that person was still on his side, if what he was doing, was in the name of Jesus. Luke 9:51-55

Attitudes in John chapters 15&16
Subjects and themes from these two chapters (plus a few verses from the chapters either side) have been grouped together. Because Jesus teachings are concentrated in these chapters.

Attitude to the present and future
I have given you my teachings so you will not take the wrong turn or have a crash 16:1

I have told you in advance what will happen, so that when it does occur, you will believe. 14:29

You only understand so much now, but you will understand more, in the future 16:12

After my crucifixion and 3 days in a tomb, your sadness will turn to happiness. 16:15-22

I have told these things so you can have peace 16:33

Jesus and his disciples

I want you to testify about me 15:27

You can be connected to me. 15:1

I want you to 'remain' connected to me.15:4

Fruit

I chose you. 15:16

I chose you to bear much fruit 15:16

I want you to bear even more fruit than you are now, which will occur, if you allow a little pruning 15:3

It is to my Father's glory, if you bear more fruit 15:8

Friends

You are my friends 15:14

Because you are my friends, everything God told me, I have told you. 15:15

The Holy Spirit

It is for your good that I go away and the Holy Spirit comes. 16:7

"When the counselor comes.." The Holy Spirit and I are working in tandem, for your good and the good of the future Church. 15:26

The Holy Spirit will testify about me 15:26

The Holy Spirit who is given to you, is like a counselor Like a friend who will give you good advice for the journey 16:7

If people are to be convicted of their sin. It will because of your words and actions but also because the Holy Spirit has been at work in their hearts convicting them. 16:8

Your friend, the Holy Spirit, will guide you into truth. When you are unsure of the truth ask your friend, the Holy Spirit to reveal it to you. That is his nature – the Spirit of truth. 16:13

God

God has given me everything 16:15

Ask God, using my name, for anything in line with his will 16: 23-26

In this chapter I have only reviewed, some of Jesus' teachings and in most of his teachings, the focus is on, the person's motive or attitude.

The Son of God

If someone were to ask a group of Christians, "why do you believe, Jesus is, the Son of God?", their replies might be various.

Christian A might reply. "He is the Son of God because he was conceived by the power of God, rather than by natural means. Further, after he was crucified he rose from the dead. That is all the evidence I require to prove that

Jesus, was the Son of God.

Christian *B* might reply. "Jesus was the Son of God because he cured every kind of sickness and he exercised authority over both demons and nature"

Christian *C* might reply. "Jesus is the Son of God because he claimed he was the Son of God. For example, when the Sanhedrin (the ruling religious council) were trying to pin a charge against Jesus, they asked him if he was "the Christ?" Jesus reply was,

"from now on, the Son of Man (the term used in the book of Daniel to describe the Messiah) will be seated at the right hand of the mighty God." They all asked, "Are you then the Son of God?"

He replied, "You are right in saying I am." Luke 22:69-70

"So" said Christian *C,* "Jesus was the Son of God because he claimed he was the Christ, and the Son of God."

Christian *D* took another tack. Christian *D* said. "Jesus was the Son of God because God confirmed that he was the Son of God. At his birth, there was a whole army of angels and a star overhead. And when Jesus was transfigured, a voice from heaven said, "This is my Son, whom I love..." Mark 9:7 NIV

Christian *E* took another tack. Christian *E* said Jesus was the Son of God because the Spirit of God who was in some people of that time caused them to recognize that Jesus was, the Son of God. For example, when John saw Jesus coming towards him, he exclaimed.

"Look, the lamb of God, who takes away the sin of the world." John 1:29 NIV

And Simeon, who the Holy Spirit had revealed to him that he would not die before he had seen the Christ. As soon as he saw Mary and Joseph bring the baby Jesus for dedication, he said.

"Sovereign Lord, as you have promised, you can now dismiss your servant in peace. For my eyes have now seen your salvation..." Luke 2:29-30

"So" said Christian *E,* "people, filled with the Holy Spirit, recognized that Jesus was the Son of God."

Christian *F,* took another tack. Christian *F* said. "Jesus was the Son of God because he fulfilled these prophecies about the Messiah.

He was born of a virgin. Isa 7:14.

During his ministry, many despised and rejected him. Isa 53:3

During his trial he did not defend himself. As the prophet Isaiah conveyed it. "As a sheep is silent before the shearers,he did not open his mouth." Isa 53:7

Before being hung on the cross, he was pierced and beaten. Isa 53: 5&6

After he was pronounced dead, he was buried in a tomb provided by Joseph or Arimathea. Only the wealthy could afford tombs hewn out of rocks, so Isaiah prophecy was correct.

"But he was buried like a criminal he was put in a rich man's grave." Isa 53:9

So concluded Christian *F,* Jesus was the Son of God because he fulfilled Old Testament prophecies about the Messiah.

Christian G, took a different tack. Christian *G* said. "You are all right (that is Christians A-F), but there is a further reason Jesus was the Son of God - the nature of his teachings!" Christians A-F were surprised at Christian *G's* comments because they thought they had covered all the bases and offered every reason to believe that Jesus was, the Son of God. i.e. They had pointed out that:

- Jesus was conceived by the power of God, and not natural means. Also, he had risen from the dead

- Jesus healed every type of sickness and had authority over both demons and nature.

- Jesus claimed he was the Son of God.

- God spoke in a voice from heaven to say, this is my Son.

- People who were full of the Holy Spirit, recognized that Jesus was the Messiah.

- Jesus fulfilled the Old Testament prophecies about the Messiah.

So as far as Christians A-F were concerned every base had been covered, and were surprised that Christian *G* thought there was an additional reason to believe, Jesus was the Son of God.

Christian *G* asked. "Do you remember how Jesus said to the Pharisees, "You are from below I am from above. You are of this world I am not of this world...." John 8:23

Evidence that Jesus is the Son of God can be found in the nature and content of his teachings. For example he was able to tell the first Sadducees who did not believe there was a heaven, that when people rise from the dead they will have bodies like the angels in heaven. Matt 22:30

Said Christian *G.* "Only someone who came from heaven, would know that when we die, we will have bodies like the bodies of angels."

In the sermon on the mount, Jesus was able to confidently tell listeners that there are no thieves in heaven, and no rust, like there is on earth. Matt 6:19-20

Because Jesus, being God's Son, had come from heaven, he was also able to say that some things applied, in both realms. For example he said, "whatever you bind on earth will be bound in heaven." Matt 1619.

And Jesus was able to confidently tell those listening to his sermons, that your heavenly father "knows" what you need. Only someone who has lived in heaven would know, what God knows! Matt 6:32

"So", continued Christian *G,* "teaching after teaching all demonstrate that Jesus had a knowledge that only the Son of God would know.

Christian *H*, had waited patiently for the other

Christians to make their point, but when Christian H got her turn, she said. You are all right in what you have said, but you have missed one further point.

"It is obvious from the nature of his teachings and the attitudes in them, that Jesus came from above. That he was not from this world. She exclaimed. Jesus gave teachings that were so, *unearthly. So, not from this world!"*

He recommended people taking the lower seats at banquets instead of the honored seats.

He recommended doing good to our enemies when every normal human knows that it is appropriate to repay them or hold a grudge against them.

He urged his followers to put the kingdom of God first rather than their own interests and let God provide for our needs.

Any normal person knows that we should worry about taking care of providing for our needs and then, after that think what God may have to say, for an hour on Sunday.

Jesus, being the Son of God, brought a divine perspective to this Earth and challenged his disciples to think like God thinks, and to live, like citizens, from another realm.

To win by losing

To get, by giving

To give, and not expect anything in return

To forgive, instead of remaining, unforgiving.

To love without borders or boundaries.

To advance in the kingdom of God by serving instead of living to advance in life

To put God's kingdom first, instead of our own interests.

To store up treasures in heaven, rather that on on Earth.

To believe that the only thing that is not impossible is something that is, impossible.

To have faith that God has everything in control and knows every need when we humans so desperately want to be in control and identify ways in which every need can be met.

"These values," said Christian *H,* ""do not come from this Earth – and the Son of God, brought them here."

Chapter 5

Faith

It was imperative to have the chapter about the king of love' in this book, because this book is about Jesus. However there was another subject that Jesus was passionate about - faith. He continually encouraged his disciples to have faith. He taught them about it, and even chided the disciples about their lack of faith.

Jesus asked this question:

> "But will the Son of Man find faith
> on earth when he returns." Luke
> 1:18 (G.N)

Faith for Jesus was not an isolated subject like studying the measurements and weight of the Statue of Liberty, or the Eiffel tower. For Jesus, faith was intrinsically tied to his understanding of who God was and is - and his relationship to Him. Jesus' faith in God revolved around three aspects of his nature. God's power. God's knowledge. God's love.

God's Power

In the Bible there were three occasions where the angel Gabriel came to this earth to tell three people that women would conceive, in seemingly impossible circumstances. Sarah, the wife of Abraham and Elizabeth the wife of Zechariah (when both were very old) and Mary the mother of Jesus, while she was still a virgin.

In all three instances, the angel Gabriel told the people involved that "nothing" is impossible with God.

When the angel Gabriel spoke to the people named in the Bible, he could no doubt read the immediate question on their minds as they asked themselves. If this type of miracle was possible and each time the angel Gabriel used the same words:

"Nothing is impossible with God."

Jesus had the same perspective as the angel Gabriel. He was 'surprised' that the first disciples and others did not/could not believe that God could do anything. As Jesus was to tell the Sadducees

> "You are in error because you do not know the Scriptures or **the power of God.**" (bold type inserted for emphasis) Matt 22:29

Because Jesus knew of God's great power, he did not have any difficulty believing that:

- Five loaves and two fishes could be multiplied to feed a crowd.

- Water could be turned into wine.

- A storm could be calmed.

- A person could be set free from demons.

- Any sicknesses healed.

- People could be raised from the dead.

- It was possible to walk on water.

Jesus tried to pass that same faith onto his disciples. He said

> "I tell you the truth, if you have faith

> as small as a mustard seed, you
> can say to this mountain. Move
> from here to there and it will move.
> Nothing will be impossible for you."
> Matt17: 20-21

Jesus challenged the twelve to have faith. After he had been teaching a crowd of 5000 people, he said to the disciples

> "You give them something to eat."
> Mark 6:37

In the next few seconds, the disciples were probably thinking to themselves, 'Jesus is off his rocker.'

It is now near the end of the day and even if we were near Jerusalem, all the bakeries in the city would be cleaned out of bread if we were to suddenly arrive and try to order enough bread to feed this crowd. But we are not anywhere near Jerusalem and yet Jesus is standing here, expecting us to feed all these people.

At that point, the disciples and Jesus probably were on different planets. The disciples were on the planet called, *seeing is believing.* While Jesus was on the planet called, *believing is seeing.*

Jesus could not see the problem for the

answer that is why he asked

> "How many loaves do you have?"
> Mark 6:38.

Jesus knew that a few loaves and fish would be enough for God to perform a miracle.

I am sure that most of us do not have any idea how great is God's knowledge, power and creative ability! Whether it is something small or great God is able to do create anything. I think of our brains which have about 86 billion neurons in them, and each has about 10,000 connections.

Can you imagine being a technician and being tasked with making ten thousand connections for each device in front of you?

Astronomers and astrophysicists are aware that the universe is being held together by some force, which they call "dark matter" – because they cannot see it or detect it.

It is a shame that the majority have not considered the Biblical explanation.

"When I look at the night sky and see the work of your finger – the moon and stars which you have set in place." Psa 8:3. To the God who arranged for each neuron to be connected ten thousand times and for the stars to be in place multiplying a few loaves and fish is as we might say today, Kid's play.

God's knowledge

Jesus not only knew that nothing was impossible to God, he was also very aware of God's intimate knowledge of every person and every situation. Jesus taught his disciples that God knows details as minute as, the number of hairs on each person or where each bird falls. He also taught them that God knows about our need for food and clothing, even before we ask.

It is unfortunate that there were no video camera's in Jesus time. When Jesus asked those listening,

> "And why do you worry about clothes...and food Matt 6: 28 & 31

there was a smile on his face. And behind that smile, was this question. Do you think these needs have escaped, God's attention?

Jesus was making the same point, two different ways. He told the disciples explicitly. "...your heavenly Father *'knows'* that you need them." Matt 6:32 Italics added for emphasis.

Secondly he pointed to examples of God's provision. Flowers with rich garments but who do not need a clothing boutique, to look beautiful. Birds who are amply fed, and yet have no stores, to buy food. Matt 6:29 & 26

God's heart
Jesus faith rested on three factors. God's limitless power. God's unlimited knowledge of every situation, and also - the goodness of God. The God who sends rain on both the righteous and unrighteous. The God who looks after little birds and who would not think of giving us a snake or scorpion, if we ask for food. Luke 11:11

Faith and...
When the disciples were with Jesus on a hillside and there was a huge crowd listening, they probably thought he had lost his senses - asking them to feed this huge crowd, in the wilderness.

They did not express their thoughts to Jesus, but probably thought it. Even if we were camped outside Jerusalem, there would not be enough bread available from the bakeries at the end of a day for a crowd of 5000 plus.

We do not know what sparked the boy standing near the disciples to act like he did. He was obviously one of those people who when they see a need, ask "What can I do to meet that need?"

It is likely that the disciples looked worried, so he thought he would help both the disciples, and Jesus out, by offering his dried fish and flat unleavened bread that his mother had insisted he take with him.

What has this to do with faith? On virtually every occasion where Jesus healed a person or delivered them from a demon, he asked them to do something.

In the Gospels, there are a few examples of people who acted in faith, even before Jesus asked them. The woman who reached through the crowds, and touched his garment. The Roman Centurion who sent a message to Jesus while he was still coming - not to bother coming,but to only, "say the word." With these two people it was not necessary for Jesus to ask them to participate in the miracle. They being people of faith, decided to act anyway.

Every other person who asked Jesus to heal them, he asked them to respond with an act of faith - in a small way. When two blind men followed Jesus and called out to him, He asked "Do you believe that I am able to do this?" Then he touched their eyes and said

> "According to your faith will it be done to you", Matt 9:27-29

Or to another man he said

> "Get up! Pick up your mat and walk." John 5:6 & 8

When Jesus could not ask for faith from the person concerned such as Lazarus, he asked for faith from Lazarus sisters. In fact Jesus usually asked two things of people who wanted to be healed:

1. "Do you want to get well?"

2. For their faith.

It has been pointed out that when the angel Gabriel spoke to Mary, he said "Nothing is impossible with God. Luke 1:37. The word the angel used was not 'for' God or 'to' God. Nothing is impossible for God or to God – but the angel used the word, "with".

That word implies that God works 'with' human beings like us, to bring about miracles. Seldom does God work a miracle separately from people. Usually it is, with people.

An example from the Old Testament is Moses..Moses was asked to hold his hand out to part the Red Sea.

That is how Jesus conducted his ministry. He had an immense faith in God but he asked the people of his time to exercise their mustard seed faith, by doing something such as. Putting out a hand. Getting up off a mat or stepping out of a boat on the water. All he asked was for mustard-seed faith – God did the rest.

There are three reasons Jesus had great faith. Jesus knew the Scriptures. Reading the Bible creates faith. Remember he said to the Sadducees. "You do not know the Scriptures or the power of God."

Secondly, Jesus spent time in prayer before every significant phase in his life. Further, Jesus was filled with the Holy Spirit from the start of his ministry and followed the Holy Spirit's leading during the course of his ministry.

In the book of Acts, Luke (the author), noted how Stephen was full of the Holy Spirit and faith. Acts 6:5

Faith is a separate subject in itself but certain factors contribute to our faith. The three factors already mentioned. Having a confident expectation that God can do a miracle. Mixing with other people of faith. Recalling times in the past when God has done a miracle in our lives.

Chapter 6

The Road to Calvary

By implication of the Churches I have worshiped in, all my Christian life, I am a Protestant, though I have never thought of myself as a Protestant or any other title except. Christian or follower of Jesus.

I have always strongly disliked categorizing Christians into branches of the Church like Protestant or Catholic. Or into theological streams like Evangelical or Conservative. Or into denominations like Presbyterian or Assemblies of God or Seventh Day Adventist or Catholic or Baptist or....

Or any other way we may categorize Christians.

Putting Christians into a particular box is an issue Paul addressed with the Christians at Corinth. Some were saying they were of Paul or Apollos or Peter or Christ. 1 Cor 1:10-17

In that passage, Paul attempted to shift their focus from key leaders of the time, to Jesus. I believe that is equally important today. That we Christians, regardless of the name of our church or denomination or branch of the Church. Keep our focus on Jesus, and not the name tag of the Church or branch of the Church. Or theological stream

> It is Jesus who matters, first and last – and any other tags should be worn lightly!

Despite having written about my dislike of tags and distinctions, for once I am going to use a tag that some use to distinguish Christians because there is a point to be made from one of those distinctions

In most Catholic Churches, there is a statue of Jesus hanging on the cross, bleeding in agony. Traditionally in Protestant Churches, the cross is empty, signifying that Jesus has risen.

Often there are lights behind the cross or the cross is white, signifying life and light.

Because of my Protestant background, whenever I have seen a statue of Jesus dying on the cross in a Catholic Church, my gut reaction has been. 'Don't these Catholics know that Jesus rose from the dead?' And secondly. Why the morbid fascination with Jesus bleeding and dying?

By contrast, we Protestants want to shout "Hallelujah, he is risen" and proclaim the victory of Jesus over death, sickness and sin - and virtually anything else we can think of.

As I have become older, and hopefully wiser I have come to the conclusion that this Protestant obsession with the victory, has swept under the carpet the pain that Jesus went through, in order to win, that victory.

It is as if we are on a Protestant express-train. An express-train that cannot wait to get to it's destination called, Glorious Resurrection! This Protestant express-train rushes through a number of stations without even stopping. To locals at these station the express train rushes through and is gone in a blink of the eye.

These stations that the express train rushes

through, have different names. Names such as:

- Betrayal (Station-master – Judas)

- Desertion (the eleven disciples)

- Scorn (Chief Priests)

- Political football (Jesus was sent from the Chief Priests to Pilate to Herod, and back to Pilate)

- Repeated denial (by a key disciple called Peter)

- Crowd baying (The turn-coat, rent-a-crowd)

- Expedient decision-making (Pilate)

- Whipping (ordered by Pilate)

- Derision (Romans soldiers)

- Darkness (It was dark while Jesus hung on the cross)

- Sin of the World on his shoulders

- PPD (Protracted painful death)

- ABC (Accompanied by criminals)

- Abandonment (by God)

All of these stations the Protestant express-train rushes through and passengers scarcely have time to read the signs, let alone stop to consider, what these names, mean.

Apart from the tradition of focusing on Jesus dying rather than his resurrection. The symbolism of a white cross, with bright lights behind it, is consistent with my personality. My natural philosophy to life is:

> "Eliminate the negative and accentuate the positive."

So to stop and consider the painful events of Jesus' trial and crucifixion, is consistent with my personality.

We Protestants have not fully understood who Jesus was and is if we have not at least tried to imagine what it was like for Jesus to go through, all of those stations.

I believe the Gospel writers spared us most of the details of the crucifixion, possibly because crucifixions occurred regularly in those times, and they thought readers would be able to picture, the slow painful death, Jesus endured.

Crucifixion by the way, was not something the Romans invented. It was a method of killing people that the Romans adopted from the cruel Assyrians. But the Romans adopted it and refined it, to make more painful. The way a person was placed on a cross, was designed to make them move, every time they needed to breathe.

And because the hands and feet were nailed to the cross it meant additional pain every time the person tried to breathe. Because movement accentuated the pain caused by the nails (spikes would be a more accurate description) through the hands and feet. A crucifixion was designed to be a slow painful death – and at the same time, a humiliating public spectacle.

Dr Arnold Fructenbaum analyzed the words that Jesus used during his ministry, and realized that Jesus always called God, "Father" or "My Father". So whoever was standing by the cross at the moment Jesus died and heard his anguished cry, "My God, my God, why have you forsaken me?", must have remembered the words exactly - because Jesus had never used those words before.

Jesus death was accompanied by dark skies and was eventually accompanied by a dark series of events involving various people.

Now I have not changed my conviction that the empty cross and the resurrection of Jesus, is the best news the Church has. But perhaps the image of Jesus suffering on the cross and his grace under those testing circumstances, is something we need to hold as close to our hearts as the resurrection, and not rush as quickly as possible between the last supper and the resurrection. Or better still. Not mention those stations, at all.

Perhaps there is a healthier position for all Christians in this. For Catholics to see the empty cross more often. A cross lit up as a sign that the cross has become a symbol of victory. And for Protestants to see the pain before the gain. Or perhaps the best description of the events to do with the cross comes from a reporter called Rob Harley. He said,

"The cross is at the intersection of despair and hope."

Those two threads run through the Easter story, despair and hope. The difficult side of the cross means that anyone who suffers rejection or betrayal or pain can say "My Lord understands those feelings intimately."

The empty cross and the empty tomb tell us that no hell on Earth is permanent. But through Jesus, there is victory over our defeats and pain. And victory over the ultimate destroyer – death.

We need to remember Jesus went through all those stations on the slow-train, for our sake, bearing our sins and our shame, to bring us into God's presence

The connection

The Jesus who was, as Isaiah predicted - . abused, beaten and rejected, is a connection-point to Jesus, for some. Over the radio, I heard this story. Specific details about this person's life have been withheld, but I will recount enough details to give readers, the picture.

As a result of a liaison between a soldier of an occupying power and a woman in that country, a baby girl was born. Because she was illegitimate, and half-foreign and half local - lower forms of men used that as an excuse to regularly, sexually abuse her.

At about 9 years of age, she was adopted by loving Christian missionaries. She became a Christian as a result of their kindness, but found it hard to put into practice the teaching of Jesus, to forgive her enemies because of the terrible abuse and rejection she received as a young girl. She was often called a "foreign devil" – as if that justified the abuse.

Among the reasons she was eventually able to forgive those who had abused her, was what she knew about Jesus, her Lord.

- Jesus was accused of being demon possessed. Mark 3:22
- She was called a "foreign devil."
- Jesus was rejected by most of the significant people in his land.
- She was rejected by many in her land.

Jesus forgave those who rejected him and eventually this girl was able to forgive the men who perpetrated evil deeds against her, because, she knew: Jesus loved for her. She also knew the caring love of a missionary couple and she knew about Jesus' example of forgiving his enemies.

Chapter 7

The Past and The Present

The story of Jesus didn't end at the cross. There was more - a resurrection and an ascension - and although I wrote in the introduction that this book is about the three years of Jesus' ministry and not about the risen Jesus, we miss out if we do not realize there is a connection between the two.

When the disciples saw Jesus ascend into heaven, suddenly they noticed two angels standing by them. The angels said

> "This same Jesus, who has been taken from you into heaven, will come back...." Acts 1:11 N.I.V

What the two angels said about Jesus, is identical what we read in the book of Hebrews.

> "Jesus Christ is the same yesterday and today and forever."
> Heb 13:8 N.I.V

So from the point of view of being a disciple of Jesus today, He is still the 'same' as he was for the first followers! The same Jesus, who first asked people to "come follow me" two thousand years ago, still calls people today to "come follow me".

Just as he befriended the first disciples and came to love them deeply. This 'same' Jesus, still wants to be a friend to you and I, and for us to know his love.

With the first disciples, Jesus looked past their sins and their faults to see their strengths and possibilities. He looked past the sins of immoral people (like Mary Magdalene) and cheats (like Zaachaeus), and doubters (like Thomas) and those fussing about detail (like Martha) and cowards (like Peter).

With these disciples, Jesus looked past their sins and personality flaws and mistakes and saw what was on their heart. He also knew their eternal worth and potential.

Jesus still does that today, with any person who chooses, to follow him.

> He looks beyond our sins, to our eternal worth.

> He looks beyond our personality flaws, to see our potential.

> He looks beyond our errors of judgment, to see what is on our heart.

Jesus looked beyond the sins of the thief hanging on the cross – to his eternal worth saying. "Today you will be with me in paradise"

Jesus looked beyond Peter's personality flaw (he was quick to say at the last supper he would never deny Jesus – but later did so,three times), to see his potential.

A woman broke a jar of perfume over Jesus head that cost a years wages. The disciples were right in saying. The money could have been used to give to the poor, but Jesus looked at her heart, and defended her saying. "She has done a beautiful thing... Mark 14:6

When the first disciples and when we mess up if we are sorry. Jesus will lovingly forgive us – and set us on the pathway, once again.

"He will not let us off, but will not let us down either."

With Peter, Jesus did not let Peter off the hook about the way he had denied him three times. After his resurrection, Jesus asked Peter three times "do you love me?" That was Jesus' loving way of reminding Peter of the three times, Peter had denied Jesus.

But there was more to Jesus than just lovingly forgiving Peter.

During that same conversation, outrageously Jesus commissioned Peter to lead the new Church with these words. "Feed my sheep" and "Feed my lambs."

Anyone else other than Jesus would probably have cold-shouldered Peter, or rebuked him - and banned him from any leadership positions for at least, 20 years. That he both forgave Peter and appointed him to be the leader of the new Church, was an act of outrageous grace.

Jesus is the same with us today. We too can make mistakes but that is not the end of the story. Jesus wants to forgive us, restore us, and put us on the pathway again so that we can be a blessing to others.

He understands you

I wouldn't go as far as saying Jesus used psychology in his relationship with people – 1900 years before there was a science called psychology but when relating to people, he J recognized that each person he encountered, was a unique individual – and what they needed to hear from him was different to others because they were, unique individuals.

Those involved in sales, leadership training and communication, have recognized that different people will information more easily, if the person communicating to them, recognizes how they are wired to best receive that information.

There are three different ways (some say four) people are wired to optimally receive information. The acronym is called VAK which stands for Visual, Audio and Kinisthetic. Visual people learn best by picture or diagrams – through what they see. Audio people respond best through what they hear and Kinisthetic people learn, by doing.

From what we read in the Gospels, it appears that Jesus was aware of how people who were his disciples were VAK wired nearly 2000 years before people recognized that people are wired to optimally receive information, by different ways.

Take Peter. He appears to be a Kinisthetic type of disciple. One who learns by doing. One day after Peter had been fishing all night, and caught nothing – Jesus told him to row his boat short distance from the shore and endeavor to catch fish.

If it had been any person, other than Jesus, Peter would have told them, where to go because he was an experienced fisherman and knew the fish he was targeting, mainly came to the surface at night and retreated to the depths, during the day.

So it would have been, only because Jesus had told him to row out during daylight, that Peter did so but I am sure that, under his breath, Peter was muttering to himself.

Jesus I know you do miracles, but I am a very experienced fisherman and so are my fellow fishermen. Night-time is the time to catch them and not day-time. You may be able to heal any sickness but you have spent your working life in a carpenter's shop, not on the lake, like me.

Jesus being the Son of God, knew there were enough fish close to shore to virtually sink Peter's boat and he also knew that Peter is the type of person who learns best, by doing. The Kinisthetic type.

Jesus knew that Peter would only recognize that he was the Son of God – and not merely a carpenter from Nazareth when, every muscle in Peter's body was straining to pull in the catch of a life-time - during the day – and there were so many fish that the net's were breaking and the boats, nearly sinking.

Then, take the two disciples on their way home to their village of Emmaeus, after Jesus body had been laid in a tomb. As far these two disciples were concerned, it was finito for Jesus. He was gone never to walk this Earth, again.

Anyone familiar with a crucifixion in which the victims body was pierced so that their blood and their life ebbed away under the watchful eyes of Roman guards, whose task was to make sure the person died – and was truly dead - before their body was lowered to the ground.

Anyone, including the two disciples who returned home to the town of Emmaeus, knew it was finito for Jesus and anyone else who was, crucified. So how was Jesus to get through to these disciples that he had risen?

Perhaps these two disciples were a combination of audio (hearing) and visual (seeing) and Kinisthetic (walking) – because Jesus chose to walk with them, and remind them of how he had told them he would die and rise again – and how this was foretold in the Scriptures.

When disappeared and they put two and two together. Not only did he walk like Jesus and talk like Jesus and look like Jesus. He was Jesus. They said to themselves. "Were not our hearts burning within us while he talked on the road and opened the Scriptures to us?" Luke 24:32 NIV

With another disciples, Jesus took a different approach. because they were different. Mary Magdalene was an audio person – one who responded to words and the tone a person used, when speaking.

So when Jesus approached her by the tomb he knew that she did not need a complete run-down of the Scriptures (the method he used with the two in the way to Emmaeus) but all she would only need to be convinced that he was risen was to hear Jesus speak her name *"Mary"*

John 20:16

With Thomas Jesus' approach was different again. Jesus recognized that Thomas was a visual person, so when the other disciples told Thomas that Jesus they had 'seen' Jesus because Thomas was a visual person and he had not seen Jesus with his own eyes he did not believe their story. For Thomas seeing, was believing!

So when Jesus appeared to Thomas he did not explain the Scriptures as did with the two on the road to Emmaeus. Or simply say his name as he did with Mary, rather. Jesus simply showed Thomas his nail-scarred hands, because he knew that seeing was important to Thomas. John 20:24-28

Jesus understood how to get the best response out of people. With the Samaritan woman at a well, the big thing with her was, knowledge. She believed that the Messiah when he came, would know information that only the Messiah – could possibly know. That is why she said, "When the Messiah comes,he will tell us everything."

So when Jesus began to tell her details about her life, even though he had never met her before or lived in her village she began to put two and two together. He must be the Messiah, she reasoned.

Jesus got the best out of Peter by showing him grace, after he denied Jesus three times. And Jesus made a disciple out of Zacchaeus not by rebuking him for his obvious sins. Or avoiding him like the religious leaders – but by doing the opposite. Inviting himself to Zacchaeus' house.

Jesus understood the people of his time, and treated them all as, unique individuals.

Now this 'same' Jesus, understands us. Understands us as unique individuals with different gifts, personalities, training and possibilities. After Jesus ascended into heaven, two angels stood there and said. "This 'same' Jesus, will return."

He understands people

Jesus not only understands us as individuals, but understood/ understands people, in general. He knew what motivated the people of his time. What controlled them and what they were seeking from life.

Jesus recognized that most people of his time were seeking, four things. Either, freedom, peace, happiness or life – and not coincidentally, Jesus offered* those four precious commodities, to his followers. Freedom, peace, happiness and life

*That is, those who applied his teachings to their lives.

However, Jesus recognized that many people of his time were seeking these goals, in ways they would never find them. By discarding moral laws. Through the accumulation of wealth. Through power. Through religious rituals, and other means.

We can see how Jesus understood people because of two phrases he used. "Do not worry" and "do not fear." And even when Jesus did not say, "do not worry" - he asked those listening. "Why do you worry?"

So why did Jesus say those words – because that is what we humans are prone to do? Worry and fear, this or that. And when Jesus e reappeared to the disciples after he had risen from the dead. Instead of saying, "do not fear." He said, "Peace.

Jesus recognized that some people of his time worried about what would happen when they died. So he addressed that concern with the words. "Do not fear.... John 14:1

Jesus recognized that the humans of his time and the human beings of every age have a tendency to worry about the present and the future. And worry about whether they will have enough food. Or whether the clothes they are wearing are fine enough.

Jesus also recognized that people of his time and people of every age think it natural to hold against those who have wronged them – and better still. Get even, with them.

Jesus came up with a revolutionary idea. Forgive them and do them good. He understood that people who hold onto resentment are the losers. Not those who wronged them.

Jesus had equally revolutionary thinking about the Romans who occupied their country. There was an unwritten law that a Roman soldier could ask any citizen to carry his Army pack for a mile – and I'm sure that most who did this bitterly resented the imposition and let the Roman soldier know about it, through non-verbal means.

The sullen look. Walking slowly. Dumping the pack on the ground as soon as the mile was up. Jesus' revolutionary idea was to offer to carry the Roman's pack, two miles instead of one.

Jesus recognized that some people in his age (and every age), swore as if that made them more important, or their words more powerful.

That is why Jesus astutely observed. "Let your yes be yes and your no be no. Anything else comes from the devil."

Chapter 8

Walking the talk.

Talk is easy. Walking the talk is more difficult. Politicians in every country have made an art-form out of saying the right thing at the right time and in the right place to impress the public and hopefully, win votes. Whether their lives match the rhetoric, is often, irrelevant.

A feature about Jesus that arrested my attention as I looked at him afresh in the pages of the Gospels, is that what he said what he did, were one and the same! In other words, he walked his talk.

The word integrity comes to mind. Even his enemies admitted

> "Teacher we know that you are a man of integrity, " Matt 22:16

When Jesus was in a heated dispute with the Pharisees over various subjects, he challenged them.

> "Can any of you prove me guilty of sin?" John 8:46

There is no doubt that if Jesus' life had not matched his teachings, his opponents would have exploited that gap, and told him so. But Jesus knew there was no gap between his walk, and his talk, that is why he challenged his enemies to come up with evidence.

Because they could not find any way of accusing Jesus of living contrary to the teachings of the Scriptures and his own teachings - they had to resort to malicious and untrue comments like…

> "you are a Samaritan and demon possessed." John 8:48

During any period of history, people love to have heroes. People today are no different. We love to have heroes. Today many authors have written about the lives of stellar sports people, movie stars, great musicians, scientists, civic leaders, politicians and military heroes.

More often than not, when the authors or journalists have taken a closer look at the lives of many of our heroes, they have found gaps between the image, and the real person. When the spot-light has been turned onto their lives, the flaws in their image or character has been revealed.

With Jesus by contrast, there was no gap between the image and the real Jesus. What he said and what he did, were one and the same. Or as we might say today "Jesus walked the talk", as the following examples illustrate.

Teaching: Love your neighbor as yourself Matt 19:19

Example:

> When Jesus saw her weeping.... Jesus wept. John 11:33-35

Teaching: I tell you the truth, if you have faith as small as a mustard seed, you can say to this mountain, move from here to there and it will move. Nothing will be impossible for you. Matt 17: 21-22

Example:

> "You of little faith, why are you afraid?"
> Then he got up and rebuked the winds
> and waves,.." Matt 8:26

Teaching: "But seek first his kingdom and his
righteousness" Matt 6:33a

Example:

> When faced with doing the will of God
> or facing a cruel death he prayed. "Yet
> not as I will, but as you will ". Matt
> 26:39

Teaching: Do not leave Jerusalem, but wait
for the gift I told you about, the gift my Father
promised. John baptized with water, but in a
few days you will be baptized with the Holy
Spirit Acts 1:4-5 (G.N)

Example:

> At the beginning of his ministry Jesus
> said. ."The Spirit of the Lord is upon
> me." Luke 4:18

Teaching: "Instead, whoever wants to be
great among you must be your servant and
whoever wants to be first must be your slave"
Matt 20:26-27a

Example:

> "After that, he poured water into a

> basin and began to wash his disciples feet, drying them with the towel that was wrapped around him." John 13:5

Teaching: Go to the Street corners and invite to the banquet anyone you find. Matt 22:9

Example:

> "While Jesus was having dinner at Matthew's house, many tax collectors and 'sinners' came and ate with his disciples" Matt 9:10

Teaching: For if you forgive men when they sin against you, your heavenly Father will also forgive you. Matt 6:14

Example:

> On the cross Jesus said

> "Father, forgive them, for they do not know what they are doing." Luke 23:34

That last example of Jesus living what he taught others to do, that is, forgiving his enemies I find especially moving. You see, I have stood on the hillside where it is believed that Jesus spoke the Sermon on the Mount, and where he taught the crowd about forgiving their enemies. That spot overlooks Lake Galilee, and you can see the lake, shimmering below.

Most readers will not know that in Israel, the skies are blue and completely clear of clouds from sunrise to sunset, for about seven months of the year. There is what they call the rainy season, but for seven whole months, if anyone is planning to do any outdoor activity (in Jesus' case – preaching), you can bank on the fact that there will be no rain or clouds, throughout the day - day after day!

So my picture of that time when Jesus spoke those words about forgiving your enemies, is this.

He was standing on a grassy hillside. Thousands were listening attentively, hour after hour. The sky was blue, and the Sun was warm on his face. Maybe there was a breeze, and the birds were singing. And below him was beautiful Lake Galilee, and to his left snow capped Mt Hermon.

Now anyone can say noble words, when everything is in their favor. When the spotlights are on you (so to speak) or in Jesus' case the Sun was shining on his face.

Anyone can say noble words when the birds are singing. When there is a gentle breeze blowing past and below is a shimmering lake and nearby there is a large, snow capped mountain.

And most important of all, crowds hanging on every word he was saying, while close by were his, devoted disciples.

The real test of a person's character is to put their words into practice not when everything is for them. But when everything is against them!

When Jesus put his words into practice, the sun-drenched hillsides of Galilee were colloquially speaking, on a different planet!

When Jesus put his words into action about forgiving your enemies, the skies were dark and the temperature cold. He had been whipped to nearly, a stand-still. His body (like all who were hung on a cross) was contorted, to maximize the pain.

Not long before that, he had been verbally abused at different times by three different groups. The religious leaders, a rent-a-crowd and Roman soldiers.

During the later part of his trial, the Roman Governor Pilate had washed his hands of Jesus and natural justice preferring the expedient route of releasing a notorious murderer because he did not want to upset the religious authorities – and the crowd.

And King Herod, for his part, had been

delighted to see this 'miracle worker' for a brief period of time for he had heard so much about Jesus. But his interest was not in Jesus welfare. Only that maybe Jesus would do a miracle while he was looking on.

And not long before Jesus put his teachings into action, one of his close disciples betrayed him (Judas) and another (Peter) denied he knew him three times. And, as for the rest, they just fled!

After a false trial, there was the humiliation of being paraded at Herod's palace. The jeering of a rent-a-crowd. The Governor washing his hands of Jesus life and then his betrayal, denial and desertion by his close disciples. Not to mention a severe whipping and nails that leached his life away.

After all that, Jesus had every reason to be 'bitter' against his disciples for betraying, denying and deserting him. Bitter against the Roman Governor for perverting the course of justice. Bitter against the religious authorities, for fighting God's purposes. Bitter against the crowd, for being swayed by the authorities and crowd emotion. And bitter, against God!

At a time when Jesus had every reason to be bitter against, so many in his society, Jesus put into practice his teaching about forgiving your enemies.

when the grassy hillsides. When glistening Lake Galilee, the chirping birds and the rapt attention of the crowds were all, seemingly a million miles away!

That contrast between the situation where Jesus taught the crowd to forgive their enemies, and the situation where he put his teaching into practice, could not have been, more opposite.

Apart from the situations being poles apart as the examples in the middle part of this chapter indicate. Jesus doing what he taught others to do was the norm in his life. That leads to this conclusion.

I am proud to be a disciple of Jesus, because of what he said. I am also proud to be a disciple of Jesus, because of what he did, but I am especially proud to be a disciple of Jesus because. Both what he said and what he did, were one and the same!

The example of Jesus leads back to the Christian life, we modern-day disciples are called to live.

> Jesus asks us to forgive our enemies (in the same way he forgave his enemies)

Jesus asks us to 'serve' (as he served)

Jesus asks us to put the kingdom of God first (in the same way he put the kingdom of God first)

Jesus asks us to love others (in the same way he loved others)

Jesus asks us to trust our life to God (in the same way he trusted his life to God)

Jesus us to trust God to meet our needs (in the same way he left his carpentry business and trusted God to provide his needs)

Jesus asks us to believe that everything is possible and no storm is so great it cannot be calmed. Or hill so high, it cannot be moved (in the same way he rebuked a storm, and brought peace)

Jesus calls to stand for truth and justice in the same way he spoke the truth and stood for justice in the Temple.

Jesus wants us to notice the glory of God's creation in flowers and nature. In the same way he noticed God's incredible handiwork.

Jesus wants us to value children in the same way, he valued children.

Jesus wants us to show grace to those

who recognized their mistakes, in the same way he offered grace to those who made mistakes.

I hope it is the desire for all Christians to be like Jesus and as indicated in the introduction, God wants us to be like Jesus. In the words of Paul.... to be conformed to the likeness of his Son. Rom 8:29 N.I.V

The Holy Spirit also wants us to be like Jesus. One of the functions of the Holy Spirit is to remind us of everything Jesus said and did. Jesus, speaking about the Holy Spirit said.

> "He will bring glory to me by taking what is mine and making it known, to you." John 16:14

Jesus wants us to be like himself, and follow in his footsteps. He said, "You are truly my disciples if you live as I tell you to. And you will know the truth and the truth will set you free." John 8:32

So the Father, Son and the Holy Spirit (and the cloud of witnesses), all want us to be like Jesus. It is our choice to say,

"Yes Lord, I want to be like you."

About Philip Watson

I have grown up and live in New Zealand - Aotearoa (the Land of the Long White Cloud), currently residing in Auckland, our largest city with a population around 2 million people.

Around half of all New Zealanders live in Auckland. It is here that I can find the time to reflect on my faith and write.

It is the Bible and an intelligent and informed explanation of it's contents, that is the wind in the sails of the books I write. I am unashamedly evangelical or charismatic in my faith and my writings.

After finishing Theological College in New Zealand, I traveled to the Middle East to walk in the footsteps of Jesus, to glean a glimpse of the life he would have lived on this earth and soak in the ambiance of the world of Jesus and the glory of God's creations. This was for me a discovery of God and how important my Christian faith is for me, my family and my life.

I enjoy telling stories in my books, informing

and educating you, the reader, on our journeys. The richness of the history of the biblical lands and the truth of the Bible has moved me to reach out in Discipleship Books Ministry, an ordinary person helping other ordinary people find their faith in Jesus Christ, our savior.

These books I have put on Amazon are the culmination of 20 years of research, discovery and worship in the Christian Church. In many ways, these books map my journey as a Christian coming to grips with the meaning of being a true follower of Christ, and how to be the best disciple of Jesus I can be.

I pray that these insights I reveal in my books can create the same positive enlightenment in you as they have in me.

www.ingramcontent.com/pod-product-compliance
Lightning Source LLC
LaVergne TN
LVHW051638080426
835511LV00016B/2382